Financial Statement and Budget Report 1995-96

Return to an Order of the House of Commons dated 29 November 1994: for

Copy of Financial Statement and Budget Report 1995–96 as laid before the House of Commons by the Chancellor of the Exchequer when opening the Budget

THE RT HON SIR GEORGE YOUNG Bt MP

Treasury Chambers, 29 November 1994

Ordered by the House of Commons to be printed 29 November 1994

LONDON : HMSO

£15-50 net

House of Commons No. 12

Contents

Chapter 1	The Budget	5
Chapter 2	The Medium-Term Financial Strategy	14
Chapter 3	The economy: recent developments and prospects	17
	Annex A: The economy in the medium term	51
	Annex B: The Panel of Independent Forecasters	54
Chapter 4	The public finances	63
	Annex A: Further analyses of the public finances	75
	Annex B: Conventions used in presenting the public finances	85
Chapter 5	The Budget tax and national insurance measures	89
	Annex A: Explaining the costings	104
	Annex B: Tax changes announced before the Budget	106
Chapter 6	Public spending	109
	Annex A: Public expenditure analyses	129
	Annex B: Departmental groupings and nationalised industries	137
List of abbreviations		139
List of charts		141
List of tables		143

1 The Budget

1.01 The economy is now recovering strongly, and inflation has fallen to its lowest level since the 1960s. The Budget is designed to ensure that the improvements in the public finances announced in 1993 are delivered, and to introduce further structural reforms to make the economy work better. This will help to ensure sustainable growth in the medium term supported by permanently low inflation.

The public finances

1.02 The tax and spending measures in the two 1993 Budgets were intended to ensure that the public sector borrowing requirement (PSBR) returns towards balance in the medium term, and the projections published last November showed it close to balance by 1998–99. The deficit on the Government's current account was projected to disappear by 1997–98.

1.03 But the economy has grown faster than envisaged a year ago, with GDP now expected to be up 4 per cent in 1994. And inflation has turned out lower, taking it well into the lower half of the Government's target range.

1.04 Faster growth will tend to bring the PSBR down more rapidly. But lower prices reduce revenues, which tends to raise public borrowing. So the Government has made substantial cash reductions in its spending plans, which are also slightly lower in real terms than a year ago. This should enable the PSBR to return to balance by the end of the decade, as intended in last year's Budget, with the public sector current account deficit eliminated by 1997–98. The new projections are summarised in Table 1.1.

Table 1.1 The public sector's finances[1]

	Per cent of GDP					
	1994–95	1995–96	1996–97	1997–98	1998–99	1999–2000
Receipts[2]	37¾	39¼	39¾	40	40¼	40¼
Current expenditure[2,3]	42	41¼	40½	39½	38¾	38
Current balance[2]	**−4¼**	**−2**	**−½**	**½**	**1½**	**2¼**
Net capital spending[2,4]	1¾	1½	1½	1¼	1¼	1¼
Financial deficit[2]	6	3½	2	¾	0	−1
Privatisation proceeds and other financial transactions	1	½	¼	¼	0	0
Public sector borrowing requirement – per cent	**5**	**3**	**1¾**	**¾**	**0**	**−1**
– £ billion	**34½**	**21½**	**13**	**5**	**−1**	**−9**

[1] *In this and other tables, constituent items may not sum to totals because of rounding.*
[2] *Figures on a national accounts basis. See Annex B to Chapter 4.*
[3] *Includes depreciation of fixed capital.*
[4] *Capital spending net of depreciation and less capital transfer receipts.*

1 The Budget

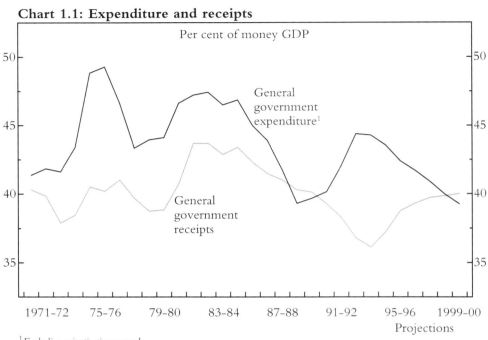

Chart 1.1: Expenditure and receipts

[1] Excluding privatisation proceeds.

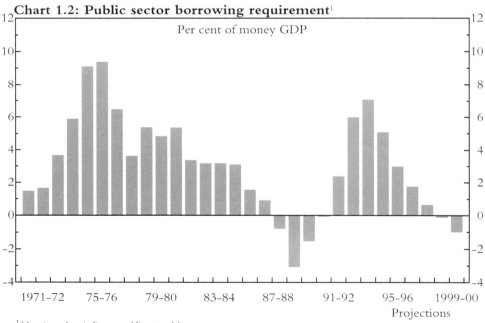

Chart 1.2: Public sector borrowing requirement[1]

[1] Negative values indicate a public sector debt repayment.

1.05 The cash reductions in spending plans are bigger than the likely reduction in receipts, so the PSBR is forecast to come down faster than before. The main changes in the projections in cash terms since the last Budget are set out in Table 1.2.

1 The Budget

Table 1.2 Changes in the projections since November 1993[1]

	£ billion			
	1995–96	1996–97	1997–98	1998–99
PSBR path in November 1993 Budget	30	21	11	2
Changes in:				
general government expenditure[2]	−8	−9	−11	−13
general government receipts[3]	−1½	−3	−5½	−8½
other items[4]	−1½	−1½	−1	+1½
Total change in PSBR	−8½	−7½	−6	−3
PSBR path in 1994 Budget	**21½**	**13**	**5**	**−1**

[1] November 1993 forecast adjusted for classification changes – see paragraph 6A.7.
[2] Excluding privatisation proceeds. See Table 4.8.
[3] See Table 4.7.
[4] A minus sign indicates higher privatisation proceeds or lower public corporations' market and overseas borrowing.

1.06 These changes are analysed in more detail in Chapter 4. Most of the reductions in general government expenditure are accounted for by reductions in the Control Total, though cyclical social security is also lower because of lower unemployment, lower prices and the measures in the Budget (see paragraph 6.73). Privatisation proceeds are also increased from 1995–96 to 1997–98. The changes in receipts are mainly accounted for by changes in the path of the economy; the medium-term effect of the Budget measures is comparatively small (see Table 4.7), though transitional relief for business rates reduces revenue in the short term.

1.07 The Budget is intended to be broadly neutral in its effects on the public finances, given the changed paths of output and inflation since last November. Higher output is reflected in a lower PSBR than in the November 1993 Budget, particularly in the next three years. The impact of the Budget measures on the public finances is summarised in Table 1.3.

Table 1.3 Budget changes in tax and spending

	£ billion		
	1995–96	1996–97	1997–98
Taxes and NICs			
changes from an indexed base[1, 2]	−1·0	−0·7	−0·4
Public expenditure			
total Budget changes in cash terms[3]	−7·2	−9·0	−9·8
total Budget changes in real terms[3, 4]	−0·9	−2·3	−2·8
[1] Of which transitional relief for business rates:	−0·6	−0·1	0

[2] See Tables 1.4 and 5.1.
[3] Changes in the Control Total since the November 1993 FSBR, adjusted for classification changes, and Budget measures affecting cyclical social security. See Table 6.2.
[4] £ billion, 1993–94 prices. See Table 6.2.

1 The Budget

The details of the Budget

1.08 The details of the Budget are set out in subsequent chapters. Chapter 2 describes the Medium-Term Financial Strategy which sets out the framework of the Government's macro-economic policy. Chapter 3 describes recent developments in the economy and the prospects to mid-1996; and an annex sets out the economic assumptions underlying the new plans for public expenditure and the medium-term fiscal projections. Chapter 4 provides projections for the public finances up to the end of the decade. Chapter 5 sets out the tax and national insurance proposals in the Budget. And Chapter 6 describes the Government's spending plans to 1997–98, with a forecast of the outturn for public expenditure in 1994–95.

1.09 Chapter 6 is inevitably less specific about Budget measures than Chapter 5, since Budget decisions on tax consist of specific measures which are the Chancellor's responsibility, whilst the decisions on spending set budgets for which other departments are responsible. The full detail of how they allocate their spending will be set out in their departmental reports.

1.10 The Budget measures are summarised in the box on pages 12–13. They contribute to the Government's strategy for strengthening the supply side. This aims to make the economy more responsive to market disciplines by enlarging the market sector, increasing competition, deregulating, and improving the climate for enterprise. There are measures to provide further encouragement to small business which have been informed by the Industrial Finance Initiative, and measures to help people back into work. The direct effects of the tax and NIC measures on government revenues are given in Table 1.4 and the new public spending plans are summarised in Table 1.5. The forecast of the public finances in 1995–96 is summarised in Table 1.6.

1.11 Chapters 4, 5 and 6 of this report set out the Government's tax and spending plans in the context of its overall approach to economic, social and environmental objectives. After approval by Parliament for the purposes of Section 5 of the European Communities (Amendment) Act 1993, it will form the basis of submissions to the European Commission under Articles 103(3) and 104c of the Treaty establishing the European Union.

1 The Budget

Table 1.4 The Budget tax and national insurance measures[1]

	£ million yield (+)/cost (−)			
	Changes from a non-indexed base	Changes from an indexed base		
	1995–96	1995–96	1996–97	1997–98
Income tax				
main personal allowance and thresholds indexed	−555	0	0	0
personal allowances for 65s and over up by £430	−200	−150	−210	−210
lower rate band increased by £200	−170	−80	−100	−110
Savings				
TESSAs – extended	★	★	−150	−160
PEPs extended to corporate bonds etc	−10	−10	−25	−40
Helping people back to work				
employer NICs – lower rates reduced by 0·6%	−235	−235	−260	−265
employer NICs – rebate for long-term unemployed	0	0	−45	−45
Investment in small businesses				
Venture Capital Trusts	−150	−150	−290	−240
Enterprise Investment Scheme – extended	−5	−5	−10	−10
CGT reinvestment relief – extended	★	★	−15	−20
Business taxation				
business rates – new transitional scheme	−605	−605	−135	−10
VAT treatment of business cars changed	−140	−140	−100	−50
higher threshold for quarterly payments of NICs/PAYE	−75	−75	★	★
relief for post-cessation expenditure	★	★	−10	−10
VAT on second-hand goods	−60	−60	−55	−55
scales for free fuel in company cars increased	20	20	25	25
Anti-avoidance measures				
VAT avoidance	340	340	335	335
other measures against avoidance	100	100	175	225
Simplification/deregulation measures	−125	−125	−120	−120
Excise duties				
alcohol – most duties frozen	−10	−110	−110	−120
tobacco – 10p on a packet of 20 cigarettes etc	15	15	15	20
road fuels – 2·5p on a litre of petrol, 3·2p on diesel	90	90	110	130
VED – £5 on cars, freeze for lorries	125	45	45	45
gaming machine licence duty	−20	−20	45	65
Other tax changes	125	140	185	175
Total effect of Budget changes	−1 545	−1 015	−700	−445

[1] The measures and their revenue effects are set out in more detail in Chapter 5.
The cost/yield of measures announced before the Budget are set out in Annex B to Chapter 5.

★ = Negligible

1 The Budget

Table 1.5 The public spending plans[1]

	£ billion						
	Estimated outturn	New plans			Changes from previous plans		
	1994–95	1995–96	1996–97	1997–98	1994–95	1995–96	1996–97
Control Total by department							
Social security[2]	70·4	73·0	76·2	79·5	1·5	0	0
Health	31·7	33·0	33·3	34·1	0	0	0
DOE – Local government	29·9	30·3	30·9	30·9	0	−0·5	−1·5
DOE – Other	9·4	8·7	8·6	8·6	−0·1	−0·6	−0·6
Scotland, Wales and N. Ireland	28·3	28·9	29·3	29·6	0	−0·4	−0·6
Defence	22·5	21·7	21·9	22·3	−0·3	−0·3	−0·2
Education	10·5	11·0	11·2	11·2	0	−0·2	−0·2
Home Office	6·3	6·4	6·4	6·6	0	−0·1	−0·1
Transport	6·1	4·4	4·4	5·1	0·3	−1·1	−0·9
Other departments	23·6	23·7	23·2	23·0	0·8	−0·3	−0·5
Local authority self-financed expenditure	11·9	11·8	12·0	12·2	1·0	0·7	0·8
Reserve		3·0	6·0	9·0	−3·5	−4·0	−4·5
Allowance for shortfall	−1·0				−1·0		
Control Total	**249·6**	**255·7**	**263·5**	**272·1**	**−1·3**	**−6·9**	**−8·3**
– real terms[3]	244·7	242·8	244·1	246·5	3·5	−0·5	−1·6
– real growth[4]	1·4	−0·8	0·5	1·0			
Cyclical social security	14·1	14·1	14·1	14·5	−0·7	−1·4	−2·2
Central government debt interest	22·1	24·5	26·0	26·2	−0·4	0·1	0·4
Accounting adjustments	9·5	10·7	12·5	12·7	0·2	0·2	0·9
General government expenditure excluding privatisation proceeds	**295·2**	**305·0**	**316·0**	**325·4**	**−2·1**	**−8·1**	**−9·1**
– real terms[3]	289·4	289·6	292·8	294·8	3·6	−0·5	−1·2
– real growth[4]	2·3	0·1	1·1	0·7			
– per cent of GDP	43½	42½	41¾	41			

[1] For definitions, rounding and other conventions, see notes in Annex A to Chapter 6.
[2] Excluding cyclical social security.
[3] 1993–94 prices.
[4] Per cent.

1 The Budget

Table 1.6 The public finances in 1994–95 and 1995–96[1]

	£ billion			£ billion	
	1994–95	1995–96		1994–95	1995–96
RECEIPTS			**EXPENDITURE**		
Income tax	64·2	70·1	Control Total	249·6	255·7
Corporation tax	20·1	26·4	Cyclical social security	14·1	14·1
Value added tax	43·3	49·0	Central government debt interest	22·1	24·5
Excise duties[2]	26·3	28·0	Accounting adjustments	9·5	10·7
Other taxes[3]	39·7	43·0	General government expenditure excluding privatisation proceeds	295·2	305·0
Social security receipts	42·5	44·5			
Other receipts	16·3	17·8			
			Privatisation proceeds	−6·3	−3·0
General government receipts	**252·5**	**278·9**	**General government expenditure**	**288·9**	**302·0**

Expenditure, receipts and borrowing

	£ billion	
	1994–95	1995–96
General government expenditure	288·9	302·0
General government receipts	252·5	278·9
General government borrowing requirement	36·5	23·1
Public corporations' market and overseas borrowing	−2·0	−1·6
Public sector borrowing requirement	**34·4**	**21·5**

[1] On a cash basis. See Annex B to Chapter 4.
[2] Fuel, alcohol and tobacco duties.
[3] Includes council tax as well as other central government taxes.

1 The Budget

The main measures

Measures to help the economy work better

- **To help people back to work**, family credit will be increased for those in full time work; payments of housing benefit and family credit will be accelerated for people taking jobs; and, in a pilot study, family credit will be paid to people without children. To help the unemployed back into work, Community Action will be extended; there will be more Work Trial opportunities; three existing pilot schemes, Jobfinder's Grant, Workwise, and 1-2-1, will become available nationally; and two other pilot schemes, Workstart and Jobmatch, will be further developed.

- **To make it cheaper to take on new staff**, employer national insurance contributions will be cut by 0·6 per cent for employees earning less than £205 a week; and they will no longer have to be paid for the first year of employment when taking on someone who has been unemployed for two years.

- **To reform training**, the Training for Work programme will be refocused with the aim of increasing the number of trainees who get jobs. Around £325 million will also be spent over the next three years on the training measures announced in the Competitiveness White Paper.

- **To improve the working of the housing market**, housing benefit will be reformed so that, whether or not rents are met through housing benefit, landlords and tenants take price as well as size and quality into account in agreeing tenancies. Scaling back income support for mortgage interest from October 1995 will transfer more of the cost of mortgage default to lenders and borrowers where it properly belongs, and also reduce the work disincentives which current arrangements create.

- **To help exporters**, ECGD average medium- and long-term premiums will be reduced by around 10 per cent. The limit on cover for important developing country markets is rolled forward and increased by £300 million in 1997–98.

- **To promote investment**, the private finance initiative is gathering speed. Private finance contracts involving around £5 billion of capital investment are expected to be let in 1995.

- **To encourage more investment in small businesses**, there are a number of proposals flowing from the Industrial Finance Initiative. A new Venture Capital Trust scheme will be introduced which will provide income tax relief at 20 per cent, and CGT reinvestment relief, on investments up to £100,000 a year in the shares of trusts which invest mainly in unquoted trading companies. Income and gains on these shares will be tax free. Improvements will be made to the Enterprise Investment Scheme introduced earlier this year.

- **To cut the regulatory burden on small firms**, the threshold for quarterly payments of PAYE and NICs will be raised to £600 a month. The VAT registration threshold will be indexed. There will be consultation on annual VAT accounting and a simplified VAT scheme for small traders.

- **To encourage personal saving**, holders of Tax Exempt Special Savings Accounts will be able to deposit up to £9,000 capital from a mature account in a new account. Personal Equity Plans will be extended to cover corporate bonds and preference shares.

Measures to restrain and re-focus public spending

The Control Total is reduced by £6·9 billion in 1995–96 and £8·3 and £8·9 billion the following two years. This is achieved by:

- **savings on most programmes** to reflect the lower level of prices;

- a concerted drive to **improve efficiency and reduce waste in Government**: cash running costs of civil departments are planned to be the same in 1997–98 as in 1993–94; provision for the rest of the public sector assumes pay increases will be offset by efficiency gains and other economies;

- measures to **restrain the growth of social security** including a reform of housing benefit. A drive against fraud and reform of income support for mortgage interest will also restrain social security spending which falls outside the Control Total;

- reductions in the **housing and roads programmes**.

At the same time, priority has been given to **health**, where spending will grow in real terms each year; the Government's achievements on **education** and **law and order** are protected; and there are extra funds for **science** and **overseas aid**. Additional resources are provided for **home insulation** and **cold weather payments** on top of last year's £1¼ billion package of extra help to pensioners and those on income related benefits to meet the cost of VAT on domestic fuel and power.

Tax measures

The tax measures in the Budget are designed to:

- **increase the main personal allowance** and income tax thresholds in line with prices. The annual exempt amount for CGT and the threshold for inheritance tax are also indexed. The lower rate tax band is increased by £200 to £3,200;

- **help pensioners** by increasing personal allowances for those aged 65 and over by £430;

- **support environmental and health objectives** by raising road fuel duties by 5 per cent in real terms and tobacco duties by 3 per cent in real terms, in line with the commitments given in last November's Budget. Duty on diesel is aligned with unleaded petrol. Vehicle excise duty for cars rises by £5. A tax on landfilled waste will be introduced in 1996 after consultation, with costs on business offset by lower employer national insurance contributions;

- **ease the transition for those businesses facing higher rates bills** in 1995–96 and beyond following the revaluation of properties. Increases in real terms will be limited to 10 per cent a year for large premises and 7½ per cent for smaller premises. Support will be funded partly by the Exchequer and partly by limiting real gains for those with lower valuations to 5 per cent a year for large premises and 10 per cent for smaller premises;

- **stop a number of** artificial schemes to avoid tax.

2 The Medium-Term Financial Strategy

2.01 The objective of the Government's economic policy is to promote sustained economic growth and rising prosperity. This requires structural policies to improve the long-term performance of the economy and a stable macro-economic environment. This chapter describes the role of macro-economic policy in achieving permanently low inflation and sound public finances.

Inflation

2.02 Economies function most efficiently in conditions of low and stable inflation. Since October 1992, the Government has had an explicit inflation objective. The aim is to keep underlying inflation (as measured by the RPI excluding mortgage interest payments) in the range 1–4 per cent and to bring it down into the lower half of this range by the end of the present Parliament. This aim is being achieved; underlying inflation is already in the lower half of the range and at its lowest levels for nearly 30 years.

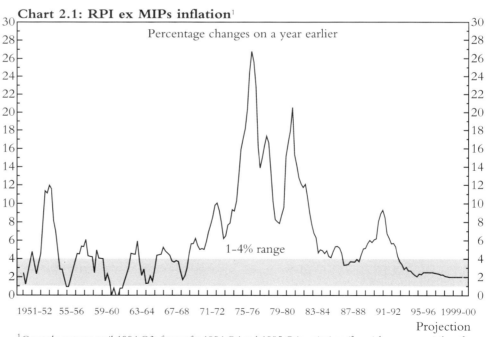

Chart 2.1: RPI ex MIPs inflation[1]

[1] *Quarterly outturns until 1994 Q3; forecast for 1994 Q4 and 1995 Q4; projections (financial year averages) thereafter.*

Monetary policy

2.03 It is the role of monetary policy to deliver low inflation. Since monetary policy influences inflation with a lag, interest rate decisions are based on an assessment of the prospects for underlying inflation in one to two years' time. This assessment is based on a wide range of information, including:

- **monetary and other financial indicators** that could provide advance warning of changes in inflation pressures. They include the growth in the narrow and broad monetary aggregates, movements in the exchange rate and asset prices, and expectations about future inflation;

- **indicators of activity** that could affect wage- and price-setting by firms and employees. If overall demand runs ahead of the economy's capacity to supply goods and services (as indicated for example by reductions in spare capacity, strong retail sales growth and labour shortages), inflation pressures may increase. The overall stance of fiscal policy is also taken into account;

- **indicators of costs** which may affect final prices directly; in particular, rises in wage costs and material input prices (including commodity prices).

2.04 Since the start of the year, the minutes of the monthly monetary meetings between the Chancellor and the Governor of the Bank of England have been published. The Chancellor's and Governor's assessments of inflation pressures and the overall conduct of monetary policy are thus much more open to scrutiny. As a result the monetary framework is now one of the most open in the world.

2.05 M0 growth has been above the top of its 0 to 4 per cent range since early 1993. This is something the Government has taken seriously. It has been a signal of faster than expected growth in overall activity. But in part it probably has also reflected the temporary effects of adjustment to lower interest rate levels.

2.06 It is also becoming evident that the recent rapid growth in M0 may reflect a potentially lasting change in its medium-term trend relative to GDP. It is likely that, in an environment of sustained low inflation and lower nominal interest rates, there is less incentive to economise on cash holdings and velocity will grow more slowly. This may imply that over the medium term M0 can grow faster than previously thought without putting the Government's inflation objective at risk. This change in trend would be consistent with experience in the 1950s and 1960s. However, it is too soon to be certain that there has been a permanent shift in trend. For much of the next year annual M0 growth is expected to remain above the top of its 0 to 4 per cent range. But growth could fall back during the year as the effects of interest rate cuts weaken, and as growth in activity moderates.

2.07 Over the last year M4 has remained in the lower half of its 3 to 9 per cent range. Growth in lending has also been very weak, as industrial and commercial companies in total have continued to repay bank borrowing. There is uncertainty about trend growth in M4 also, which can be affected substantially by changes in financial innovation (as has happened in the US recently).

2.08 Given these uncertainties, the Government will retain for the time being the existing medium-term monitoring ranges for M0 and M4. It will continue to assess the growth of narrow and broad money alongside the evidence of all the other indicators. The monitoring ranges will however be reviewed carefully in the light of continued experience.

Fiscal policy

2.09 The role of fiscal policy is to ensure sound public finances. The Government's fiscal objective is to bring the PSBR back to balance over the medium term, and the November 1993 Budget set the public finances on a path to achieve this.

2.10 Aiming for budget balance is a prudent objective given the considerable uncertainties about medium-term prospects. It allows some safety margin against unfavourable developments and ensures that the ratio of public sector debt to GDP, and hence the burden of debt service, will fall over time.

2.11 As the PSBR returns toward zero, the general government financial deficit will fall below the reference value of 3 per cent of GDP set out in the European Union's excessive deficits procedure and the public sector's balance on current account will move into surplus. On the main projection set out in Chapter 4 below, these "milestones" will be passed in 1996–97 and 1997–98 respectively.

2.12 The Government is committed to reducing public expenditure as a proportion of national income. It does not have a target for capital spending, which is now more clearly distinguished in the public sector accounts. However, the Government intends that a steadily rising proportion of capital investment in the public services should be financed by private capital, based on a proper transfer or sharing of risk.

3 The economy: recent developments and prospects

Summary

World economy   **3.01** Growth in the seven major countries (G7) picked up in the second half of 1993 and has increased further this year. It is forecast to be 2¾ per cent both in 1994 and 1995. G7 consumer price inflation is expected to rise to 3 per cent.

Output   **3.02** In the UK, GDP growth has been stronger than forecast in the summer. It is now forecast to be 4 per cent in 1994, slowing to 3¼ per cent in 1995 largely as a result of slower growth of North Sea output.

Inflation   **3.03** Underlying RPI inflation has been a little lower than anticipated in the summer and was 2 per cent in October. It is forecast to rise to a temporary plateau of 2½ per cent while prices adjust to higher commodity prices and profit margins increase in the buoyant manufacturing sector.

Labour market   **3.04** Unemployment, as measured by the claimant count, has fallen by 455,000 since December 1992 to 2½ million. The Labour Force Survey shows a similar rate of decline and suggests that rising employment accounts for most of the fall in unemployment.

Current account   **3.05** The current account deficit was much lower in the first half of 1994 than was generally expected. It is forecast to fall from £10½ in 1993 to £4 billion in 1994 as a whole and to £3½ billion in 1995.

Financial conditions   **3.06** The sterling index has been fairly steady this year. The forecast is based on the conventional assumption that sterling remains close to recent levels. Long-term interest rates have risen sharply this year, but have fallen back a little recently. Short-term rates were increased from 5¼ per cent to 5¾ per cent in September. M0 growth has continued above its monitoring range; M4 growth is in the lower half of its monitoring range.

Public finances   **3.07** The PSBR in 1993–94 was £45½ billion. It is expected to fall to £34½ billion in the current financial year and to £21½ billion in 1995–96; £3 billion and £8½ billion respectively lower than in the last Budget (after allowing for classification changes).

Medium-term projections   **3.08** For the purposes of medium-term fiscal projections, GDP growth from 1996–97 is assumed to average 2¾ per cent a year. Inflation as measured by the GDP deflator is assumed to fall from 3¼ per cent in 1995–96 to 2 per cent by the end of the decade.

The world economy

Activity

3.09 Output has continued to accelerate in the G7 as a whole. G7 GDP grew by 3 per cent at an annual rate in the first half of 1994, up from 1¾ per cent in the second half of 1993. Recovery is at last underway in mainland Europe. In the United States growth has moderated a little from its peak at the end of last year but the economy continues to expand rapidly. In Japan it is still not clear that recovery has taken a firm hold.

3.10 G7 growth is forecast to be 2¾ per cent in both 1994 and 1995, increasing to 3 per cent in the first half of 1996. After fast growth in the US and slow growth in Europe and Japan over the past year, growth rates within the G7 should converge in 1995. The US is forecast to grow in 1995 by around 3 per cent, down from nearly 4 per cent in 1994. Mainland Europe is expected to accelerate, with growth of 3 per cent in Germany and in Europe as a whole. In Japan sustained growth is expected to resume in the second half of 1994 and to average 2½ per cent in 1995.

Table 3.1 The world economy

	Percentage changes on a year earlier			
		Forecast		
	1993	1994	1995	1996 H1
Major seven countries[1]				
Real GDP	1¼	2¾	2¾	3
Domestic demand	1	2¾	2¾	2¾
Industrial production	0	3½	3¾	3¼
Consumer price inflation[2]	2¾	2½	2¾	3
World trade in manufactures	3	9¼	8¼	8¼
UK export markets[3]	0	8	7½	7½

[1] *G7: US, Japan, Germany, France, Italy, UK and Canada.*
[2] *Final quarter of each period. For UK, RPI excluding mortgage interest payments.*
[3] *Other countries' imports of manufactures weighted according to their importance in UK exports.*

World trade

3.11 World trade has picked up sharply in 1994, particularly in Europe. It is forecast to grow by over 9 per cent in 1994 – more than three times faster than in 1993 – and to continue growing rapidly in 1995 and the first half of 1996. UK export markets will probably grow a little more slowly because trade in Europe – our main export market – is projected to rise more slowly than trade between the Asian economies.

3 The economy: recent developments and prospects

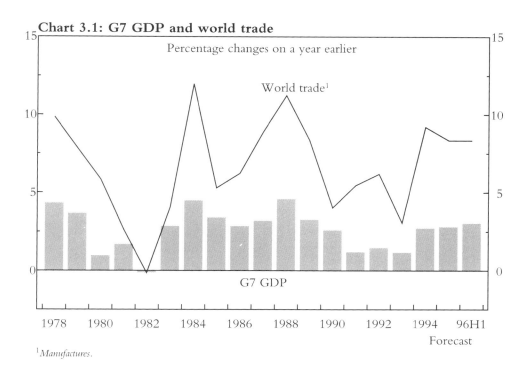

Chart 3.1: G7 GDP and world trade

[1] *Manufactures.*

Commodity prices

3.12 Non-oil commodity prices have risen by around 40 per cent since their trough in mid-1993. This sharp increase reflects both rising demand and problems of supply for some commodities. But prices have flattened off in recent months and are expected to grow more moderately over the forecast period. The Brent oil price has risen from a low point of $13½ a barrel at the beginning of 1994 and has been trading around $17 a barrel recently. It is assumed to remain around this level in the forecast period.

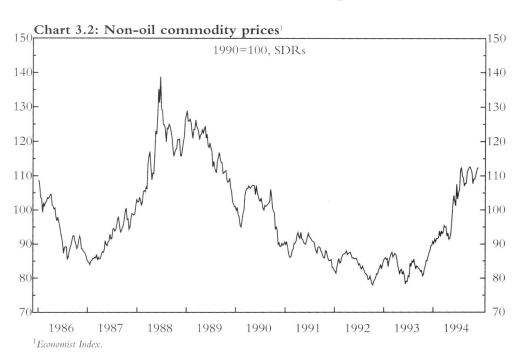

Chart 3.2: Non-oil commodity prices[1]

[1] *Economist Index.*

Interest rates 3.13 The US Federal Reserve has increased the Federal Funds rate by 2½ percentage points since it began to tighten policy in February. The German discount rate has remained at 4½ per cent since May. In Japan the Official Discount Rate has been unchanged at 1¾ per cent since September 1993. Long-term rates drifted up over the summer in all the major countries following the sharp rise earlier in the year.

Inflation 3.14 Although consumer price inflation looks to have stopped falling in the G7 as a whole, immediate inflationary pressures appear weak. In Germany inflation – now just below 3 per cent – is expected to fall further. In Japan consumer prices are stable. In the US inflation rose to 3 per cent in the early autumn but has subsequently fallen back. However, with higher commodity prices and higher output, G7 inflation is forecast to increase a little, reaching 2¾ per cent by the end of 1995 and 3 per cent in the first half of 1996.

Chart 3.3: G7 long-term interest rates and inflation

[1] Weighted average of 7-10 year government bond gross redemption yields.
[2] Growth in weighted average of consumer price indices.

Demand and output

Recent developments 3.15 In the UK output has risen more than expected in the summer. Growth in the second and third quarters of 1994 was stronger than forecast and growth in earlier quarters has been revised up. In the year to the third quarter GDP is currently estimated to have increased by 4·2 per cent; for non-North Sea GDP[1] the increase was 3·7 per cent.

---

[1] GDP excluding oil and gas extraction.

3 The economy: recent developments and prospects

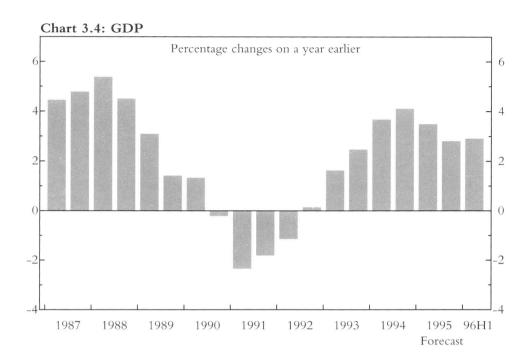

Chart 3.4: GDP

3.16 GDP is now 7 per cent above its trough in the first quarter of 1992 and 3¼ per cent above its previous peak in the second quarter of 1990. Excluding oil and gas extraction, which has risen by over 50 per cent since 1990, GDP is 6¼ per cent above the trough and 2¼ per cent above its previous peak. Output has risen in all the main sectors of the economy: by 6¾ per cent in manufacturing and 4 per cent in construction, though output is still below its previous peak in both these sectors. Service sector output, which accounts for 60 per cent of the total and fell less than output in other sectors in the recession, has risen 6¾ per cent since its trough and is now well above its previous peak.

3.17 Over the past year the basis of the recovery has shifted away from consumer demand towards exports. In the early stages of recovery most of the growth in GDP came from consumer spending. Stocks and exports also contributed, but the contribution of exports was more than offset by rising imports. Arithmetically, therefore, net trade made a negative contribution. But more recently the growth of consumers' expenditure has slowed, exports have accelerated and imports decelerated. Net trade accounts for about half the growth in 1994 so far.

3.18 Non-North Sea GDP has been growing faster than trend since the middle of 1993. The current size of the output gap – the difference between actual and trend levels of GDP – cannot be estimated with any certainty, but there is almost certainly still a sizeable gap. In other words there is still spare capacity in the economy as a whole. This should allow the economy to continue growing faster than trend without significant upward pressure on prices.

3 The economy: recent developments and prospects

Capacity utilisation 3.19 The only direct measures of capacity utilisation are based on surveys and relate to particular sectors. The CBI survey, which reflects utilisation of both labour and capital, shows capacity utilisation in manufacturing back to normal levels. Outside manufacturing, the British Chambers of Commerce and Building Employers' Confederation surveys show increases in capacity utilisation in services and construction respectively, but to levels well below those seen in the late 1980s.

3.20 However, there are grounds for thinking that currently reported levels of utilisation represent less of a constraint on expansion and hence less of an inflationary threat than in the past. Under pressure to cut costs, companies have probably been exploiting opportunities to use their existing capacity more efficiently. There have been strong incentives to reduce the time plant and machinery spends idle and to remove bottlenecks. On the employment side, labour market reforms have discouraged labour hoarding. In these circumstances the key question is how quickly capacity can be expanded and at what price. For new plant and machinery lead times on installation have probably shortened. Moreover there is a large pool of available labour: unemployment remains high despite its rapid fall since the end of 1992. Nor is there much evidence of shortages of skilled labour.

Prospects 3.21 The pace of GDP growth is likely to slow a little from now on, while remaining above its trend rate. This largely reflects much slower growth of North Sea output following the very large increases of the past couple of years. But it also reflects a marginal slowing in non-North Sea growth, mainly accounted for by slower growth of public expenditure in volume terms and little further contribution from stockbuilding.

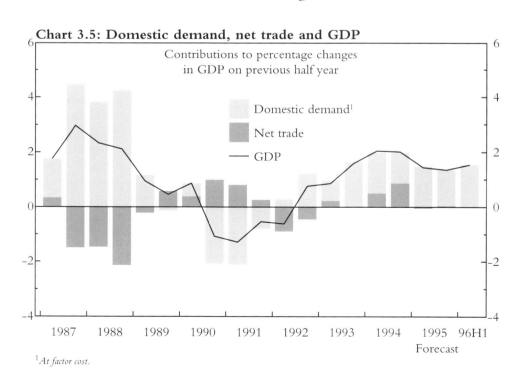

Chart 3.5: Domestic demand, net trade and GDP

[1] At factor cost.

3.22 GDP is forecast to increase by 4 per cent in 1994, and by 3¼ per cent in 1995 – stronger than the Summer Economic Forecast of 2¾ per cent in each year. Excluding North Sea output, GDP is projected to rise by 3½ per cent in 1994 and by 3¼ per cent in 1995. These growth rates are above estimates of trend growth, implying a further narrowing of the output gap.

The personal sector

Consumer spending   **3.23** The growth of consumers' expenditure has weakened this year, with quarterly growth rates of 1 per cent in the second half of 1993 giving way to increases of around ½ per cent in the first three quarters of 1994. In part this reflects greater caution on the part of consumers towards major purchases. Spending on cars has slowed, and weakness in the housing market has held back expenditure on other durable goods. Elsewhere there is much less evidence of any significant weakening since the tax rises in April, and the trend in retail sales remains buoyant. Consumers' expenditure as a whole is expected to rise by 2½ per cent in 1994.

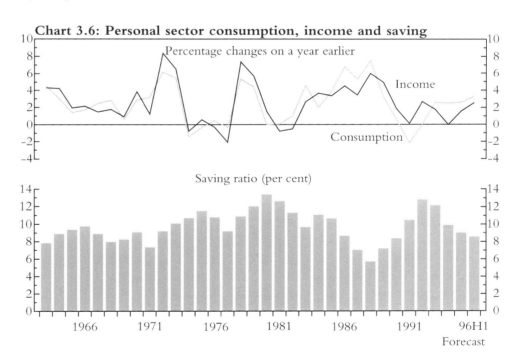

Chart 3.6: Personal sector consumption, income and saving

Saving   **3.24** As expected the saving ratio has fallen. It is estimated to have averaged 10 per cent in the first three quarters of this year, down from 12¼ per cent last year. Three related factors probably account for this fall:

- lower interest rates, lower inflation and economic recovery have encouraged spending;
- the personal sector has significantly improved its financial position by running substantial financial surpluses, which have more than offset the deficits of the late 1980s;
- consumers are to some extent offsetting the effect of higher taxes on spending by reducing their saving.

3 The economy: recent developments and prospects

Prospects 3.25 In 1995 as a whole consumption may increase by 2½ per cent, the same as in 1994. This is faster than the growth of real personal disposable income, which is forecast to rise by 1½ per cent. Thus the saving ratio is expected to fall again, though by less than in 1994 when real personal disposable income seems likely to be unchanged on 1993.

The housing market 3.26 Housing market turnover increased strongly in 1993 but has fallen back this year. House prices have moved erratically with no pronounced trend up or down. In October they were at much the same level as a year earlier. This lacklustre performance looks surprising in the face of low mortgage rates, low house prices in relation to incomes, and the continued recovery in the financial position of the personal sector. It may be the consequence of persistent negative equity and significant, though diminishing, repossessions – both unknown before the last few years. The two percentage point increase in the cost of fixed rate mortgages, the result of the rise in bond rates, may also have kept some purchasers out of the market. (Fixed rate mortgages have accounted for the greater part of new mortgage lending this year.) Finally the housing market may also still be adjusting to the changes in mortgage interest relief announced in the last two Budgets.

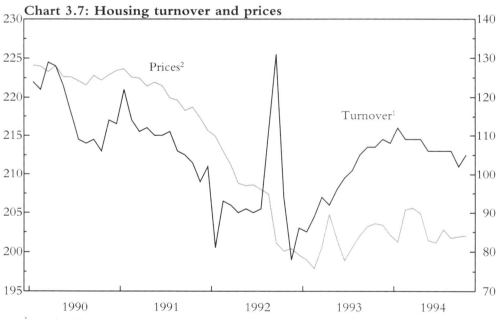

Chart 3.7: Housing turnover and prices

[1] Particulars delivered, thousands, right-hand scale.
[2] Halifax index, 1983=100, left-hand scale.

3.27 On balance the housing market indicators point to renewed recovery. Housing remains very affordable, with house prices and mortgage interest payments both low in relation to incomes. Continued economic growth, which increases the personal sector's resources and reduces uncertainty about the future, should lead to modest increases in both turnover and house prices next year.

3 The economy: recent developments and prospects

Chart 3.8: Housing affordability

[1] 1990=100, right hand scale.
[2] Per cent of first time buyers' average income, left-hand scale. 1994 average of first 3 quarters.

3.28 A prominent feature of the recession was the move by the personal sector from deficit into substantial financial surplus, as saving was increased and investment cut. The surplus fell slightly in 1993, but it remained at a historically high level. It is forecast to fall sharply in 1994 mainly because of lower saving. Further, smaller, declines are forecast for 1995 and 1996, but the personal sector is expected to remain in comfortable surplus.

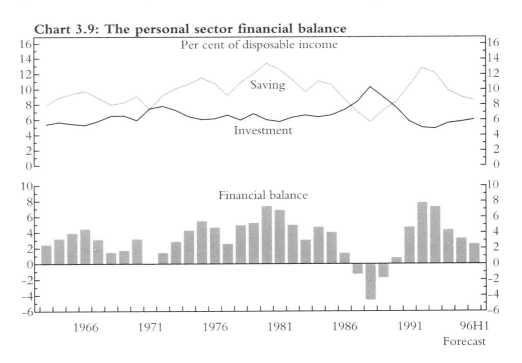

Chart 3.9: The personal sector financial balance

The corporate sector and investment

3.29 Industrial and commercial companies (ICCs) have transformed financial deficits of the order of 4 per cent of GDP in 1989 and 1990 into a record surplus in the first half of 1994. Strong profits growth, sharp reductions in interest and tax payments, and lower capital expenditure have all contributed to this dramatic turnaround. At the same time companies have been restructuring their balance sheets by issuing equity and repaying bank borrowing. The key issue for the forecast is whether balance sheet adjustment has largely been completed. One view is that most companies still have a long way to go in repairing damage to their balance sheets because recent financial surpluses fall well short of making good the large deficits run between 1988 and 1992. On this view companies will remain reluctant to invest and will continue to run relatively large surpluses.

3.30 An alternative view, on which the forecast is based, is that companies have largely completed the adjustment. Since early 1991 ICCs have repaid over £19 billion of bank borrowing and the market has absorbed large-scale capital issues. Debt as a proportion of total financial liabilities has fallen sharply, and financial assets, particularly liquid assets, have been built up. Overall the market value of ICCs, as measured by their net financial liabilities (including equity), was almost 50 per cent higher in mid-1994 than at the end of 1990. All this suggests that companies in aggregate are now in reasonable financial shape and have little need to forgo profitable investment opportunities for the sake of sustaining substantial financial surpluses.

Profits **3.31** ICCs' profits rose by 13½ per cent in 1993, having been virtually static throughout the recession. In the first three quarters of 1994 they showed a further gain of over 16 per cent on a year earlier. This reflects continued tight control over unit costs, rising output and expansion of margins, particularly for exports. Higher profits have fed through to company saving (retained income), which rose by over a third in 1993 and has continued to grow at a similar rate in 1994.

3.32 Profitability, as measured by the real rate of return on capital, is likely to show another healthy rise in 1994. Some further increase is forecast for 1995. But with output growth slowing and only modest further rebuilding of margins, profits growth is unlikely to be sustained at recent rates. Moreover dividends and, particularly, tax payments are forecast to rise relatively quickly in response to the earlier strong growth of profits. Company saving could, therefore, be fairly flat in 1995.

3 The economy: recent developments and prospects

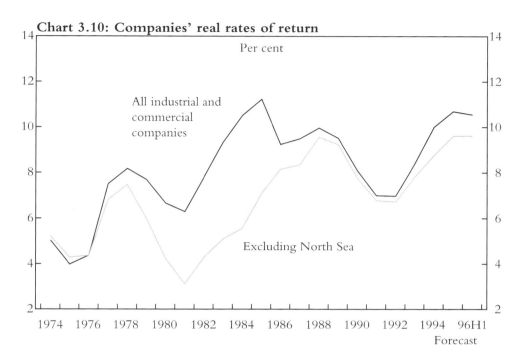

Chart 3.10: Companies' real rates of return

Business investment

3.33 Business investment in the third quarter of 1994 is estimated to have been 1¼ per cent higher than a year earlier. With profitability up, and demand and capacity utilisation continuing to rise, the need to install extra capacity is likely to become an increasingly important motive for investment. Companies should typically be well placed to finance investment internally, having moved into substantial financial surplus and largely restructured their balance sheets. So the climate for investment is much improved. Moreover there is little sign that the rise in long-term interest rates earlier this year will prevent a significant rebound in capital spending. The first indications of a marked step up in investment intentions have recently been emerging from business surveys.

Chart 3.11: Business investment/GDP ratio[1]

[1] Business investment includes public corporations, except National Health Trust hospitals.

3.34 In 1994 business investment is expected to increase only modestly, by 2 per cent. However, it is forecast to grow by nearly 11 per cent in 1995. At some point during economic upswings it is usual to see a surge in business investment: in the early 1980s this started in 1984, three years into recovery, about the same stage as 1995 in the present upturn.

Government investment

3.35 General government investment in fixed assets rose by 5¾ per cent in 1993 and is projected to rise by 4½ per cent in 1994, boosted in both years by the temporary relaxation of the rules governing spending out of local authority capital receipts announced in the 1992 Autumn Statement. As this temporary measure unwinds, local authority investment will return to more normal levels. Central government investment is also forecast to level off in 1995, following strong growth in recent years. Consequently general government investment is expected to fall back in 1995 and the first half of 1996, while remaining well above the levels seen in the 1980s.

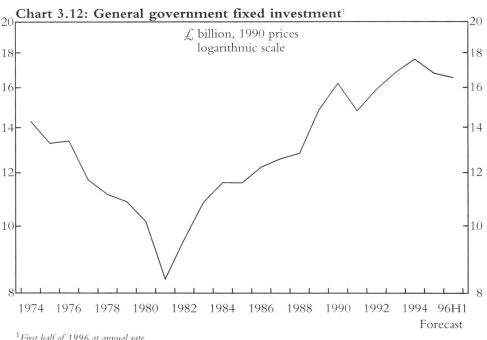

Chart 3.12: General government fixed investment[1]

[1] First half of 1996 at annual rate.

Whole economy investment

3.36 Fixed investment in the economy as a whole is forecast to grow by 3¾ per cent in 1994 and by 5¾ per cent in 1995. Stronger business investment is partly offset by weaker growth in housing investment and the fall in general government investment.

3 The economy: recent developments and prospects

Table 3.2 Gross domestic fixed capital formation at constant prices

| | | Percentage changes on a year earlier | | |
| | | | Forecast | |
	1993	1994	1995	1996 H1
Business[1]	-2½	2	10¾	9
Private dwellings and land[2]	4½	8¼	¾	8¼
General government[3]	5¾	4½	-4½	-4½
Whole economy	¼	3¾	5¾	6¾

[1] Includes public corporations, except National Health Trust hospitals.
[2] Includes net purchases of land and existing buildings for the whole economy.
[3] Excludes net purchases of land and existing buildings; includes National Health Trust hospitals.

Stockbuilding 3.37 In 1993 the level of stocks in total was virtually unchanged, though manufacturers destocked for most of the year. So far in 1994 companies have been rebuilding stocks, and stockbuilding is forecast to contribute ½ percentage point to GDP growth in the year as a whole. Stockbuilding is forecast to continue at around recent rates, making virtually no contribution to GDP growth in 1995.

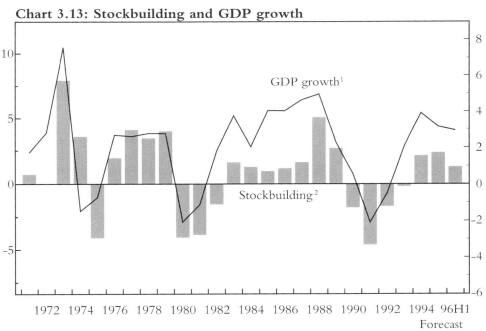

Chart 3.13: Stockbuilding and GDP growth

[1] Percentage changes on a year earlier, right hand scale.
[2] £ billion 1990 prices, left hand scale. First half of 1996 at annual rate.

Companies' financial balance

3.38 Rising capital spending against a background of slower profits growth and higher tax payments implies a declining financial balance. ICCs' financial surplus is forecast to fall from 2¼ per cent of GDP in 1994 to 1 per cent in 1995.

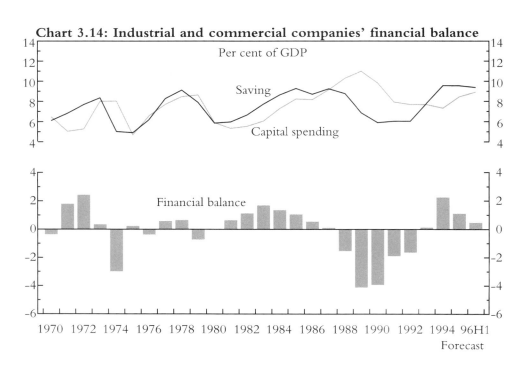

Chart 3.14: Industrial and commercial companies' financial balance

The labour market

Employment

3.39 Interpreting developments in the labour market is made difficult by discrepancies in estimates of employment[1] between the Labour Force Survey (LFS) and the employer-based survey, especially for men. According to the LFS, which is a survey of households, the trough in employment occurred in winter 1992–93, and by summer 1994 employment had risen by 334,000, with the increase split fairly evenly between men and women. But according to the employer-based survey employment has increased by only 44,000 since its trough in March 1993, with male employment having fallen.

---

[1] *Employees plus self-employed (GB).*

3 The economy: recent developments and prospects

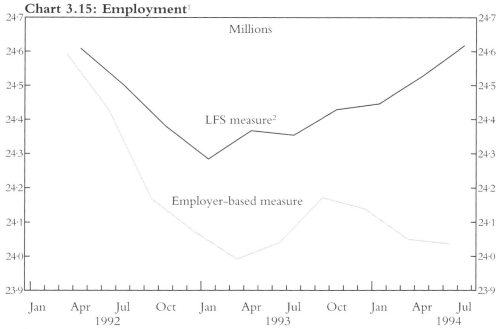

Chart 3.15: Employment[1]

[1] GB employees plus self-employed.
[2] LFS data recorded against central month of each LFS quarter.

3.40 Some discrepancy is not surprising as the two series are not attempting to measure exactly the same thing. For example, the LFS counts people in employment while the employer-based survey counts jobs. Nevertheless over the past year they cannot be readily reconciled by adjusting for known coverage differences. Of the two measures, the LFS seems more consistent with what has been happening to unemployment and output. If employment had not been increasing, the fall in unemployment would imply a large decline in labour market participation, which would not be easy to explain. At the present stage of the cycle participation normally increases.

Productivity
3.41 Uncertainty about what has been happening recently to employment carries over to the published data for productivity, and hence unit wage costs. These are currently calculated using the employer-based, not LFS, estimates of employment. Recorded non-North Sea productivity growth has yet to show any sustained slowdown, contrary to what might have been expected two and a half years into recovery. Indeed it rose by 3½ per cent in the year to the second quarter of 1994, somewhat faster than the 3 per cent recorded in 1993. This could reflect the acceleration of output in the first half of 1994, though if employment is under-recorded recent productivity growth is overstated by the published figures. But the 6 per cent rise in manufacturing productivity in the year to the third quarter is probably reasonably accurate, because the data problems lie largely outside the manufacturing sector.

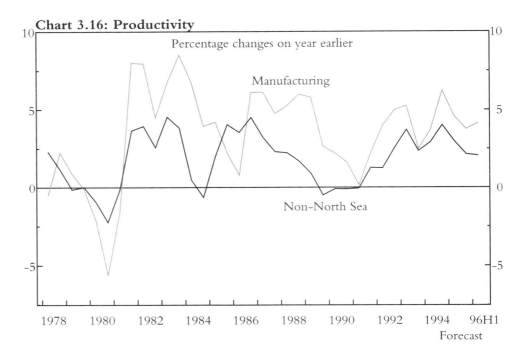

Chart 3.16: Productivity

3.42 Productivity growth in both the manufacturing sector and the non-North Sea economy as a whole is forecast to revert towards trend rates in 1995. This is usual once recoveries become more mature, and consistent with companies operating at a satisfactorily high level of labour utilisation.

Unemployment **3.43** Unemployment has continued to fall at a fairly rapid rate. Again there are two alternative measures, but they both tell much the same story. The LFS measure (on the internationally agreed definition) shows a fall of 273,000 in unemployment in Great Britain from its peak in winter 1992–93 to summer 1994. Over the same period the GB claimant count fell 334,000. The main differences in coverage between these measures are that LFS unemployment includes non-claimants who are looking for work, and the claimant count includes a similar number of people who are not classified as unemployed in the LFS. The latest LFS figures show a slower rate of decline since the spring than the claimant count, which is consistent with rising participation. This is the normal pattern as economies continue to expand, with more people being encouraged to seek work.

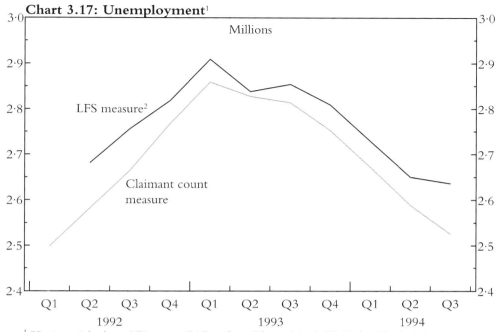

Chart 3.17: Unemployment[1]

[1] GB; time periods relate to LFS quarters: Q1-December to February (winter); Q2-March to May (spring); etc.
[2] LFS unemployment data not available on a quarterly basis until spring 1992.

3.44 Total claimant unemployment in the UK was 2·52 million in October 1994, 455,000 down on its peak at the end of 1992. Over the past six months it has fallen by 27,000 a month on average, rather faster than the average monthly decline of 21,000 a month since the peak. Looking ahead, improving job prospects, demographic factors and the new Incapacity Benefit medical test are likely to increase the number of people participating in the labour market. This means that unemployment is likely to fall less than employment rises.

Trade and the balance of payments

3.45 The current account deficit has declined sharply this year. In the second quarter it was £0·7 billion, the lowest figure since 1987. Much of this improvement arose from a stronger invisible surplus, with net investment income at its highest ever level. The visible deficit also fell, largely the consequence of higher oil output. But more recently the non-oil balance has shown a noticeable improvement too. In the three months to August the non-oil deficit was £3·1 billion compared with £3·6 billion a year earlier.

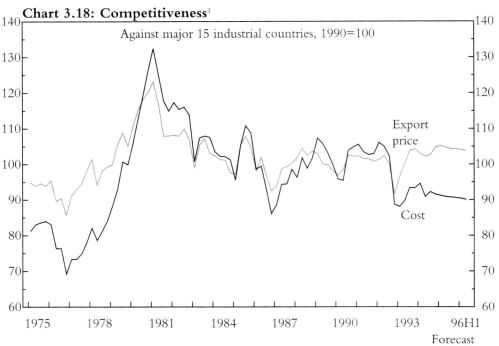

¹Ratios of UK export prices or unit labour costs to those of its major competitors; a fall means competitiveness has improved.

Competitiveness 3.46 The recent improvement in the performance of non-oil visible trade is in part the result of better competitiveness:

- The improvement in cost competitiveness following sterling's withdrawal from the ERM has been largely maintained. Cost competitiveness is currently estimated to be more than 10 per cent better than in the second quarter of 1992. Changes in unit labour costs in the UK are projected to be much the same as overseas, implying that, if the exchange rate stays close to recent levels as assumed, the current level of competitiveness will be broadly maintained.

- Taken at face value the published figures suggest that export price competitiveness is worse than before sterling left the ERM. However, it seems likely that there is a discontinuity in the export price series at the beginning of 1993 when the Intrastat system for recording European Union trade was introduced. Making some allowance for this, export price competitiveness is probably close to its pre-ERM exit level.

3 The economy: recent developments and prospects

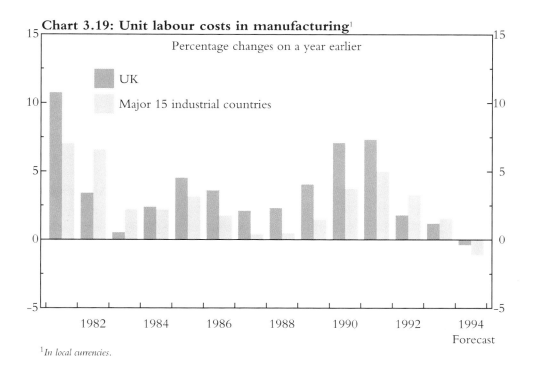

Chart 3.19: Unit labour costs in manufacturing[1]

Percentage changes on a year earlier

[1] In local currencies.

3.47 The differences between cost and price competitiveness result mainly from the rebuilding of profit margins by UK exporters. These were squeezed sharply during sterling's membership of the ERM, when firms held export prices down in the face of rising costs. Margins regained their pre-ERM levels by the third quarter of this year, although the discontinuity in export prices means that published figures probably exaggerate the increase. Higher margins encourage firms to supply the export market, and this appears to be more than offsetting any reduction in demand for UK exports because of higher prices. Recent figures for manufacturing export volumes and survey indicators of the state of firms' order books do not suggest any fall off in overseas demand for UK goods – quite the reverse. The export orders balance in the November CBI Survey was at its highest level since March 1988. While margins are not expected to grow any further, the favourable prospects for unit labour cost growth in the UK mean that the incentive to export should remain strong, notwithstanding increases in other costs.

3 The economy: recent developments and prospects

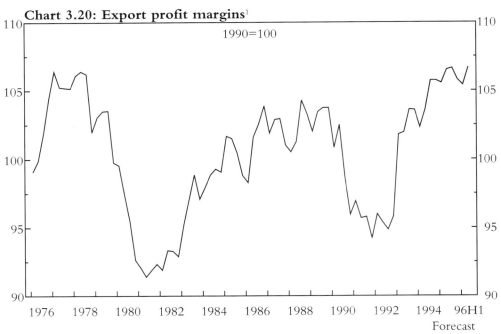

Chart 3.20: Export profit margins[1]
1990=100

Forecast

[1]Ratio of manufacturing export prices to estimated manufacturing costs.

Exports

3.48 Exports of non-oil goods increased by 10½ per cent in volume terms in the three months to August compared with a year earlier. This strong growth was well spread across categories. Non-oil exports to other European Union countries rose by 14 per cent, comfortably in excess of market growth. UK exports to other countries rose by 5½ per cent in the three months to October compared with a year earlier. Exports overall appear to have increased faster than UK export markets. This gain in share is consistent with a positive effect from improved cost competitiveness and higher margins.

3.49 The prospects remain good. UK export market growth, forecast to be 8 per cent in 1994, is expected to be around 7½ per cent in 1995, as stronger growth in Europe largely replaces weaker demand growth from North America. Exports of manufactures are expected to rise by 9½ per cent in 1994, and they more than maintain their improved market share in 1995, increasing by 8 per cent. Non-oil exports in total are expected to grow at a similar rate.

3 The economy: recent developments and prospects

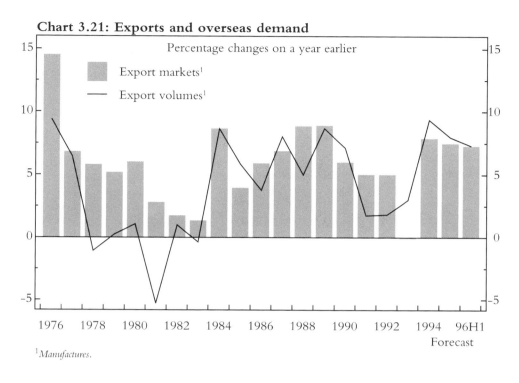

Chart 3.21: Exports and overseas demand

¹Manufactures.

Imports 3.50 Non-oil import volumes have been subdued this year. They were lower in the three months to August than in the first quarter, even though demand increased. Compared with a year earlier they have risen by 5½ per cent. Non-oil imports are expected to be 5¼ per cent higher in 1994 than in 1993. This is a modest increase in relation to the anticipated demand growth of 4 per cent – normally imports have grown 3 to 4 per cent faster than demand, the consequence of continuing specialisation of world production. This improved import performance is probably the result of better competitiveness in the UK. It is expected to continue, with import growth of 6 per cent in 1995, around 2½ percentage points faster than demand.

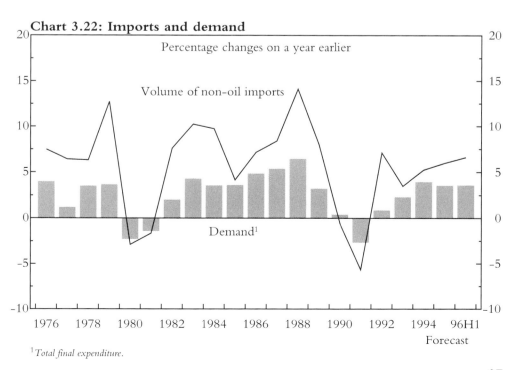

Chart 3.22: Imports and demand

¹Total final expenditure.

Trade prices 3.51 Export prices have risen sharply since sterling left the ERM as margins have been rebuilt, although as already noted the published figures may overstate the increase (see paragraphs 3.46 and 3.47). Even so, recorded export prices have not increased as much as import prices. Thus the non-oil terms of trade are 2 per cent below pre-ERM exit levels, with import prices up 15¼ per cent and export prices up 13 per cent. While the rise in export prices is largely accounted for by higher margins, the rise in import prices is more than accounted for by the impact of the lower exchange rate and the growth of world prices. Non-oil import prices are expected to rise by around 2¼ per cent in 1995, a little less than in 1994 partly because of slower growth in commodity prices. Export prices are forecast to rise by around 3 per cent in 1995, much the same as domestic producer output prices but a little faster than competing world prices.

Table 3.3 Non-oil visible trade

	Percentage changes on a year earlier					£ billion
	Volumes		Prices[1]			Non-oil visible balance
	Exports	Imports	Exports	Imports	Terms of trade[2]	
1993	2¼	3½	10¼	8¼	2	−15½
Forecast						
1994	9½	5¼	1½	2¾	−1¼	−13½
1995	7¾	6	3	2¼	¾	−11½
1996 H1	7	6½	1¾	1¾	0	−12

[1] *Average value indices.*
[2] *Ratio of export to import prices.*

The North Sea 3.52 North Sea output in the third quarter of 1994 was nearly half as high again as at the start of 1993. In 1994 as a whole it is expected to be 27 per cent higher than in 1993. But growth of less than 2 per cent is forecast for 1995 because most of the major new developments are now on stream. The increase in output has benefited the current account. Despite a fall of about 9 per cent in the sterling oil price, the oil balance is expected almost to double between 1993 and 1994, rising from £2½ billion to £4½ billion. A small further increase is expected in 1995.

Invisibles 3.53 The surplus on invisibles increased sharply in the first half of 1994 to £3½ billion, £1 billion more than in the second half of 1993. This was more than accounted for by higher investment income (the earnings on the UK's net holdings of overseas assets) which rose to over £4 billion, the highest figure ever recorded. Although figures for investment income are notoriously erratic and prone to revision, outturns over the past couple of years suggest it should continue to make a significant contribution to the surplus on invisibles.

3 The economy: recent developments and prospects

3.54 Despite a weak outturn in the second quarter of 1994, the prospects for the balance of services are also favourable. It should benefit from improved competitiveness and the recovery in world activity. The overall surplus on invisibles is expected to fall back to around £3½ billion in 1995 from £5 billion in 1994, with the turnaround more than accounted for by erratic movements of investment income.

Table 3.4 The current account

	£ billion					
	Manufactures	Oil	Other	Total visibles	Invisibles	Current balance
1993	−8	2½	−7½	−13	3	−10½
Forecast						
1994	−6½	4½	−7	−9	5	−4
1995	−5½	5	−6	−6½	3½	−3½
1996 H1[1]	−6	5	−6	−7	3½	−3½

[1] At an annual rate.

Current account **3.55** The current account deficit is expected to more than halve from £10½ billion in 1993 to £4 billion in 1994. It is forecast to fall a little further in 1995 to £3½ billion. The improvement in 1994 is largely the result of a fall in the visible deficit. A further fall in the visible deficit more than accounts for the projected fall in the current account deficit in 1995.

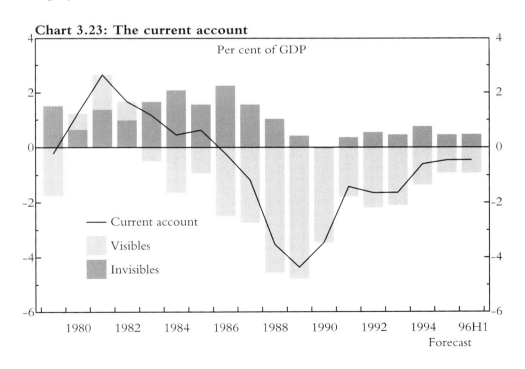

Chart 3.23: The current account

Pattern of financial balances

3.56 With the financial surpluses of both the personal and ICC sectors projected to decline, the financial surplus of the private sector as a whole is forecast to fall to 3¾ per cent of GDP in 1995 and 2 per cent of GDP in the first half of 1996. This compares with surpluses of around 6 per cent in both 1993 and 1994. The main counterpart is a lower public sector deficit, consistent with the substantial fall in the PSBR. The current account deficit is expected to fall from around 1¾ per cent of GDP in 1993 to about ½ per cent in 1994 and to remain at that level in 1995 and the first half of 1996.

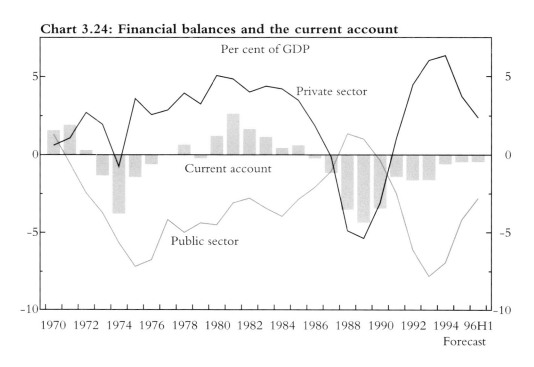

Chart 3.24: Financial balances and the current account

Financial developments

Exchange rates 3.57 Sterling has remained stable against a basket of currencies this year, although it has appreciated against the dollar and depreciated against the main European currencies and the Yen. For the most part the sterling index has been in the range of 79 to 81, averaging a little over 80 in recent weeks.

Chart 3.25: Sterling exchange rate index

Interest rates 3.58 Base rates were reduced by ¼ percentage point to 5¼ per cent in February. In September, as the strength of the recovery became evident, and to ensure that no risks were taken with inflation, base rates were raised by ½ percentage point to 5¾ per cent. Other short-term rates have followed a similar pattern: variable mortgage rates are back at the same level as a year ago, having been ¼ percentage point or so lower in the first half of 1994; deposit rates have moved similarly.

3 The economy: recent developments and prospects

3.59 Long rates rose steadily in the first half of the year. This was to a large extent prompted by developments abroad, especially in the US, which led to a rise in bond rates world wide. UK rates initially rose by more than other G7 countries' rates, but they have been declining recently and the differential with other G7 rates has narrowed. Yields on ten-year gilts, which peaked at 9¼ per cent in mid-September, are now 8¾ per cent. The future rates of inflation implicit in gilt yields remain well above most forecasts of inflation. Although the rise in long rates may have contributed to the renewed weakness in the housing market (see paragraph 3.26), there is no evidence that it has been a significant drag on recovery in other sectors.

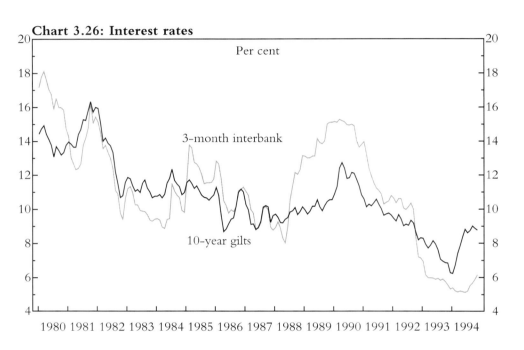

Chart 3.26: Interest rates

Asset prices   **3.60** House prices have moved erratically over the past couple of years. They are currently around the same level as a year ago. The commercial property market is in the early stages of recovery, though rents and capital values remain very depressed. Equity prices rose sharply in 1993 and in early 1994 before falling back with the decline in world bond markets. Since the spring they have fluctuated with no apparent trend. In late November they were about 15 per cent below their peak in February and little changed from a year ago. The dividend yield is about 4 per cent.

3 The economy: recent developments and prospects

Monetary aggregates

3.61 The 12-month growth rate of M0 was 7·3 per cent in October. It has been above its 0 to 4 per cent medium-term monitoring range since the start of 1993. A period of rapid M0 growth is normal when interest rates are reduced as the public adjusts its cash holdings to reflect their lower cost in terms of interest forgone. M4's 12-month growth rate was 3·8 per cent in October. So far this year it has remained in the range 3¾ to 5½ per cent, below the middle of its medium-term monitoring range of 3 to 9 per cent.

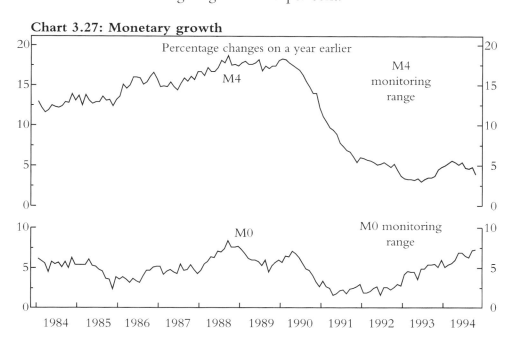

Chart 3.27: Monetary growth

Credit

3.62 The growth of M4 lending – bank and building society lending to the UK private sector – has continued to be weak. In October its 12-month growth rate was 3·8 per cent – the highest figure for the year to date. Lending secured on residential property has been growing more rapidly – its 12-month rate has been over 6 per cent. But industrial and commercial companies, as they have moved from financial deficit to surplus and taken opportunities to exploit cheaper forms of finance, have continued to repay bank debt.

Inflation

3.63 The economy now appears to be running with less spare capacity than previously expected, particularly in the manufacturing sector, implying less disinflationary pressure. Yet underlying inflation, as measured by the RPI excluding mortgage interest payments (MIPs), has continued to fall by more than forecast, recently reaching a 27-year low of 2 per cent.

3.64 Taken together, these factors suggest little overall change in the balance of inflationary pressures, compared to the assessment made in the Summer Economic Forecast. While there may be a small pick-up next year, inflation is expected to remain low by historical standards. Despite increasing capacity utilisation, there is still scope for output to expand without posing a serious inflationary threat (see paragraphs 3.19 and 3.20).

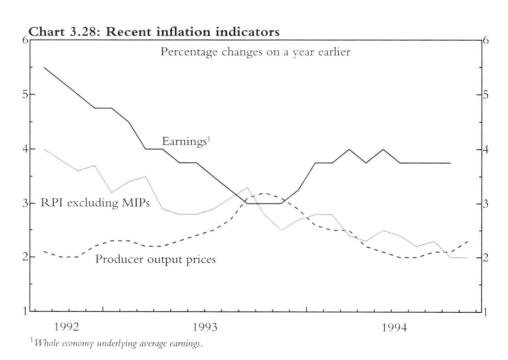

Chart 3.28: Recent inflation indicators

[1] Whole economy underlying average earnings.

3.65 However, in the shorter term the buoyancy of the manufacturing sector is likely to afford opportunities for manufacturers to rebuild margins further. In addition, there is upward pressure on costs from higher commodity prices. Producer output price[1] inflation has already started to show signs of picking up. As these effects feed through, underlying RPI inflation is expected to rise temporarily from its current very low level. But the rise is expected to be limited by the intensity of competition in the retail sector.

---

[1] All references to producer prices exclude the food, beverages, tobacco and petroleum industries.

3 The economy: recent developments and prospects

Earnings 3.66 Underlying average earnings growth picked up from its low of 3 per cent in autumn 1993 to 3¾ per cent in January this year. Since then it has remained remarkably flat, only occasionally rising to 4 per cent in months when earnings were temporarily boosted by high bonus and overtime payments. Moreover settlements generally are still very low, although they have been edging up over the past year. Latest data from the CBI show settlements in the third quarter of 2·9 per cent in manufacturing and 3·4 per cent in services, both about ¾ percentage points up on the fourth quarter of 1993. No doubt rising demand, good productivity performance and increased profits have relieved some of the pressure on companies to contain earnings, while allowing them to keep unit labour costs under tight control.

Costs and producer prices 3.67 Unit wage costs in the non-North Sea economy are estimated to have risen by only ¾ per cent in 1993, and to have barely changed at all in the year to the second quarter of 1994. These figures may be somewhat flattering if the employer-based estimates of employment (to which they are linked) have been under-recording job creation over the past year to the extent suggested by the LFS (see paragraph 3.41). Nevertheless, unit wage cost performance has undoubtedly been impressive.

3.68 This is particularly true in the manufacturing sector, where the data are more reliable. Manufacturing unit wage costs have been falling: in the third quarter of 1994 they were 1·4 per cent lower than a year earlier. They also seem likely to be lower in 1994 as a whole, following a small rise in 1993. This probably explains why producer output price inflation continued to fall through to the summer, when it reached 2 per cent. But with a sharp increase in input prices, up 7·1 per cent in the year to October, and with manufacturers seeking to increase domestic margins, output prices have already picked up in recent months. The annualised three-month rate of producer output price inflation in October was 3½ per cent, up sharply from its low point of 1 per cent in April.

3.69 Looking ahead, unit labour cost growth is likely to pick up a little as productivity growth slows down and earnings growth increases. Moreover manufacturers are expected to take advantage of buoyant markets to push through further increases in domestic margins. Some may also be looking to pass on higher imported input and other raw material costs, despite offsetting effects from unit labour costs. Price expectations as measured by the CBI survey certainly point to further upward movement in output prices in the months ahead. As a result, producer output price inflation is forecast to rise temporarily to 3¼ per cent by mid-1995. It is expected to fall back to 2¼ per cent by mid-1996, as upward pressure on margins eases and import cost inflation recedes.

3 The economy: recent developments and prospects

Table 3.5 Retail and producer output price inflation

	Percentage changes on a year earlier				
			Forecast		
	1993 Q4	1994 Q4	1995 Q2	1995 Q4	1996 Q2
RPI excluding MIPs	2¾	2	2¼	2½	2½
Producer output prices[1]	3	2½	3¼	2¾	2¼

[1] *Excluding the food, beverages, tobacco and petroleum industries.*

Retail prices

3.70 Underlying RPI inflation was 2 per cent in October, and is now expected to average 2 per cent in the fourth quarter of 1994. This is ½ percentage point below the Summer Economic Forecast, and 1¼ points below last November's Budget forecast. It is forecast to rise to 2½ per cent by the end of 1995, mainly as a result of higher producer output price inflation. The forecast rise in underlying RPI inflation is, however, much less pronounced than for producer output price inflation, because competition in retailing is expected to remain tougher than in the more buoyant manufacturing sector.

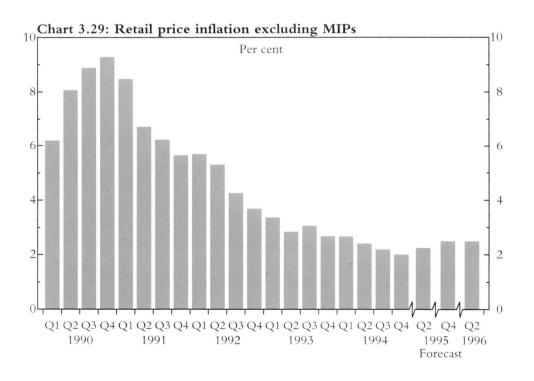

Chart 3.29: Retail price inflation excluding MIPs

3.71 The recent increase in interest rates and the further reduction in mortgage interest relief in April 1995 will tend to keep all-items RPI inflation above the underlying rate. But the outlook for the all-items rate will also depend on what happens to interest rates from now on. Other things being equal, each 1 percentage point change in mortgage rates changes the level of the all-items RPI by just over ½ per cent.

GDP deflator 3.72 Prospects for the GDP deflator differ from those for retail prices primarily because of its wider coverage. It is forecast to rise by 2 per cent in 1994–95, 2 percentage points less than in the last Budget forecast. Most of this downward revision reflects the outturns for the first two quarters of the financial year which show domestic prices, particularly for investment, growing more slowly and the terms of trade slightly less favourable than previously forecast. In 1995–96 the GDP deflator is forecast to increase by $3\frac{1}{4}$ per cent. This acceleration is expected to be temporary and mainly reflects a rebound in investment prices from extremely low levels and the projected rise in the terms of trade.

Risks and uncertainties

3.73 All forecasts are subject to risks and uncertainties. Average errors from past forecasts, shown in Table 3.8, are one illustration of their possible extent. The errors increase the further ahead the forecast looks. Obviously errors on any individual forecast may be larger than the average.

3.74 The forecast of GDP growth in 1994 has been revised up by $1\frac{1}{4}$ per cent since the Summer Economic Forecast and by $1\frac{1}{2}$ per cent since the last Budget. The inflation forecast has been revised down, by $\frac{1}{2}$ per cent since the Summer Economic Forecast, and by $1\frac{1}{4}$ per cent since the last Budget. The forecast of the current account deficit in 1994 was the same in the Summer Economic Forecast as in last November's Budget, but has now been revised down significantly. The forecast of the PSBR in 1994–95 has been progressively revised down but only by £$3\frac{1}{2}$ billion in total since the last Budget.

Table 3.6 Recent Treasury forecasts

	Percentage changes on a year earlier unless otherwise stated		
	1993 November Budget	1994 Summer Economic Forecast	1994 Budget
Gross domestic product (1994)	$2\frac{1}{2}$	$2\frac{3}{4}$	4
RPI excluding mortgage interest payments (1994 Q4)	$3\frac{1}{4}$	$2\frac{1}{2}$	2
Current account (1994, £ billion)	$-9\frac{1}{2}$	$-9\frac{1}{2}$	-4
PSBR (1994–95, £ billion)	38	36	$34\frac{1}{2}$

The Panel of Independent Forecasters

3.75 A further indication of the forecast uncertainties can be obtained from the range of views of members of the Panel of Independent Forecasters. For example, the Panel's forecasts of growth in 1995 range from 2½ per cent to 3¾ per cent and its forecasts of inflation at the end of 1995 range from 2 per cent to 4 per cent. The Treasury forecast of growth in 1995 is a little above the Panel average, though the Panel's forecasts were completed before the latest upward revisions to GDP data. The Treasury forecasts of inflation and the current account deficit are slightly lower than the average of the Panel's forecasts. The Panel's views are set out in more detail in Annex B.

Table 3.7   Treasury and Independent Panel[1] forecasts

	Percentage changes on a year earlier unless otherwise stated					
	1994			1995		
	Treasury	Independent Panel		Treasury	Independent Panel	
		Average	Range		Average	Range
Gross domestic product	4	3½	3½ to 3½	3¼	3	2½ to 3¾
RPI excluding mortgage interest payments (fourth quarter)	2	2¼	2 to 2¼	2½	3	2 to 4
Current account (£ billion)	−4	−5	−6½ to −3½	−3½	−5	−12 to 2
PSBR (financial year, £ billion)	34½	34	29¾ to 36½	21½	25	17 to 32

[1] *Submitted to the Chancellor of the Exchequer on 2 November; see Annex B for further details.*

3 The economy: recent developments and prospects

Table 3.8 Summary of economic prospects[1]

	Percentage changes on a year earlier unless otherwise stated			
		Forecast		Average errors from past forecasts[2]
	1993	1994	1995	
GDP and domestic demand at constant prices				
Domestic demand	2¼	3	2¾	1½
Consumers' expenditure	2½	2½	2½	1¾
General government consumption	1	1¼	¼	1
Fixed investment	¼	3¾	5¾	4
Change in stockbuilding[3]	¼	½	0	½
Exports of goods and services	3	8¼	7	2¼
Imports of goods and services	2¾	4¾	5¼	3½
Gross domestic product	2	4	3¼	1½
Non-North Sea GDP	1¾	3½	3¼	1¼
Manufacturing output	1¼	4¼	4¼	1¾
Balance of payments current account				
£ billion	−10½	−4	−3½	7
per cent of GDP	−1¾	−½	−½	1
Inflation				
RPI excluding mortgage interest payments (fourth quarter)	2¾	2	2½	1
Producer output prices (fourth quarter)[4]	3	2½	2¾	1
GDP deflator at market prices (financial year)	3	2	3¼	1¼
Money GDP at market prices (financial year)				
£ billion	639	678	720	
percentage change	5¾	6	6¼	2
PSBR (financial year)				
£ billion	45½	34½	21½	10½
per cent of GDP	7	5	3	1½

[1] Data in this chapter are consistent with the output, income and expenditure estimates and other series for the period to the third quarter of 1994 released by the Central Statistical Office (CSO) on 18 November 1994. The CSO will not be publishing full national accounts estimates until 22 December 1994, but revisions to available data have been carried through by the Treasury to further series, such as personal saving and sectoral financial balances.
[2] Average absolute error in autumn forecasts over past ten years: they apply to forecasts for 1995 unless otherwise indicated.
[3] Per cent of GDP.
[4] Excluding food, beverages, tobacco and petroleum industries.

Table 3.9 Gross domestic product and its components

	Consumers' expenditure	General government consumption	Total fixed investment	Stock-building	Domestic demand	Exports of goods and services	**Total final expenditure**	*Less* imports of goods and services	*Less* adjustment to factor cost	*Plus* statistical discrepancy[1]	**GDP at factor cost**
	£ billion at 1990 prices, seasonally adjusted										
1993	348·8	116·9	96·6	−0·2	562·1	140·6	702·6	153·3	72·5	−0·7	476·2
1994	357·5	118·5	100·2	2·2	578·3	152·2	730·5	160·4	74·8	−0·6	494·7
1995	366·8	118·8	106·0	2·4	593·9	162·7	756·7	168·9	77·0	−0·5	510·3
1993 1st half	172·8	58·2	48·0	0	278·9	69·2	348·2	75·6	36·1	−0·2	236·2
2nd half	175·9	58·7	48·6	−0·1	283·2	71·3	354·5	77·7	36·4	−0·4	240·0
1994 1st half	177·8	59·1	50·0	0·6	287·5	74·9	362·4	80·0	37·2	−0·3	244·9
2nd half	179·7	59·4	50·2	1·5	290·8	77·4	368·1	80·4	37·6	−0·3	249·8
1995 1st half	182·0	59·4	52·2	1·4	295·0	80·1	375·2	83·3	38·2	−0·3	253·5
2nd half	184·8	59·3	53·8	1·0	298·9	82·6	381·5	85·6	38·8	−0·3	256·9
1996 1st half	188·0	59·2	55·7	0·7	303·6	85·1	388·7	88·1	39·5	−0·3	260·8
	Percentage changes on a year earlier[2]										
1993	2½	1	¼	¼	2¼	3	2¼	2¾	2¼	−¼	2
1994	2½	1¼	3¾	½	3	8¼	4	4¾	3¼	0	4
1995	2½	¼	5¾	0	2¾	7	3½	5¼	2¾	0	3¼
1996 1st half	3¼	−¼	6¾	−¼	3	6¼	3½	5¾	3½	0	3

[1] *Expenditure adjustment.*

[2] *For stockbuilding and the statistical discrepancy, changes are expressed as a percent of GDP.*

Annex A to Chapter 3
The economy in the medium term

3A.1 This Annex describes the assumptions for output growth and inflation on which the medium-term fiscal projections presented in Chapter 4 are based. It also summarises the economic assumptions which underlie the public expenditure figures in Chapter 6.

Output   **3A.2** The illustrative paths for output and inflation are set out in Table 3A.1. At an average of 2¾ per cent a year, the growth of non-North Sea GDP remains a little above trend – estimated to be 2 to 2½ per cent a year – over the medium term. This implies that the margin of spare capacity gradually falls, with output returning to around trend levels by the end of the period.

Table 3A.1   **Output growth and inflation**[1]

	1994–95	1995–96	1996–97	1997–98	1998–99	1999–2000
Output						
Non-North Sea GDP	3¾	3	2¾	2¾	2¾	2¾
Total GDP	4	3	2¾	2¾	2¾	2¾
Prices						
GDP Deflator	2	3¼	2½	2¼	2	2
Money GDP	6	6¼	5¼	5	4¾	4¾
Memo:						
RPI ex MIPs[2]	2¼	2½	2½	2¼	2	2

[1] *Percentage changes on previous financial year; forecasts for 1994–95 and 1995–96 and assumptions thereafter.*
[2] *Percentage change in year to 1994 Q4 and 1995 Q4; percentage change on previous financial year thereafter.*

Inflation   **3A.3** With continuing spare capacity in the economy in the next few years, downwards pressure on inflation is maintained. The increase in the GDP deflator is assumed to fall to 2 per cent by 1998–99. Its path is consistent with RPI excluding MIPs inflation in the lower half of the Government's 1 to 4 per cent target range.

Annex A to Chapter 3: The economy in the medium term

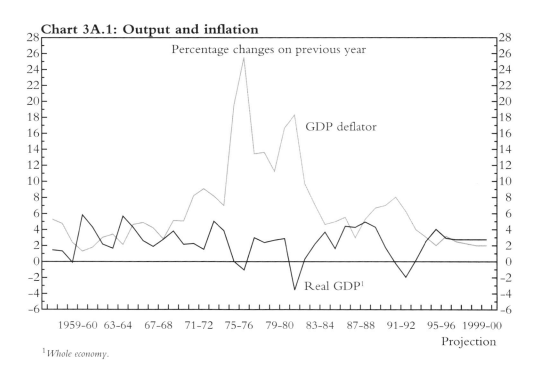

Chart 3A.1: Output and inflation

Percentage changes on previous year

[1] Whole economy.

Changes since the last MTFS

3A.4 Table 3A.2 compares the medium-term economic projections with those in the November 1993 MTFS. The table shows that output has been higher and inflation lower than expected in 1994–95. The small downward revision to the rate of output growth in the medium term is in part a consequence of this – some of the spare capacity has been used up so there is less room for non-inflationary growth over the medium term.

Table 3A.2 Differences from November 1993 MTFS projections

	Percentage points				
	1994–95	1995–96	1996–97	1997–98	1998–99
Real GDP growth					
Non-North Sea	1½	¼	–¼	–¼	–¼
Total	1½	¼	–¼	–¼	–¼
Inflation					
GDP Deflator	–2	–½	0	0	0

Assumptions for planning public expenditure

3A.5 The economic assumptions used in the public expenditure plans are set out in Table 3A.3. The assumptions that underlay the November 1993 spending plans are also shown. The assumptions for the GDP deflator in 1994–95 and 1995–96 are consistent with the short-term forecast described above. Those for later years, and all other figures, are assumptions not forecasts.

Table 3A.3 Economic assumptions for public expenditure

		Percentage changes on a year earlier unless otherwise stated			
		1994–95	1995–96	1996–97	1997–98
GDP deflator	1994 Budget	2	3¼	2½	2¼
	November 1993 Budget	4	3¾	2½	
Retail prices index[1] (September)	1994 Budget	2·2	3	2½	
	November 1993 Budget	3¼	3¼		
Rossi index[1] (September)	1994 Budget	1·8	2¼	2¼	
	November 1993 Budget	3¼	3		
Average earnings	1994 Budget	3½	4½		
	November 1993 Budget	4			
GB unemployment (millions)	1994 Budget	2·46	2·4	2·4	2·4
	November 1993 Budget	2·75	2·75	2·75	2·75
Northern Ireland unemployment (thousands)	1994 Budget	96	95	95	95
	November 1993 Budget	105	105	105	105

[1] *Used for projecting social security expenditure in the following financial year.*

Annex B to Chapter 3
The Panel of Independent Forecasters[1]

Short-term economic outlook

Monetary and fiscal projections

3B.1 Our forecasts use different projections of economic policy, which do not necessarily coincide with the policy recommendations we make.

- Our projections of **short-term interest rates** depend to a large extent on our forecasts of growth and inflation. Minford and Congdon expect weak inflationary pressure, and project rates to remain broadly unchanged over the short term. The rest of us see rates rising to 7–7½ per cent by the end of 1995 in the face of rising inflationary pressures and against a background of rising world rates.

- We assume the Government's **fiscal** stance will be broadly unchanged from the latest tax and expenditure plans, though our projections differ in detail. These details are set out below in the discussion of the PSBR.

3B.2 Our forecasts of short-term interest rates continue to be substantially lower than forward market rates, currently 8½ per cent at the end of 1995. But it is possible that these rates embody significant risk premia; central expectations of analysts in the markets appear to be within the range of our forecasts. It is less clear what interest rate expectations are built in to economic behaviour – obviously people taking out fixed rate mortgages are paying the full market rate, including any risk premium, but people with floating rate debt (the vast majority) may be expecting rates to be lower than those in the forward market. Which level of interest rate expectations is built into economic behaviour will affect the response of the economy to current and future levels of interest rates.

The world economy

3B.3 We expect G7 GDP growth to be about 2½–3 per cent in 1994 and 1995, with inflation remaining close to 2½ per cent. Commodity prices seem to be slowing after the strong growth earlier this year and remain at historically very low levels compared to the prices of manufactured goods. We foresee moderate increases in commodity prices from now on, but note the risk of higher inflation from this source.

UK overview

3B.4 The economy has continued to evolve favourably since our last meeting in May. GDP grew 3½ per cent in the year to the third quarter, underlying inflation has fallen to 2 per cent, unemployment has continued to fall, and the balance of payments has improved dramatically. Even excluding the buoyant North Sea oil sector, output has risen 3¼ per cent over the past year. In general, these developments have been a good deal more favourable than we expected a year ago. Minford considers this to be evidence of supply-side improvement. But the rest of us would caution against drawing this conclusion – the data may simply reflect the benefits of devaluation at an opportune stage of the economic cycle, when a large degree of spare capacity staved off the inflationary effects of a lower pound; we see the experience of Sweden and Italy, which have benefited from devaluation in a similar way to us, as supporting this view.

---

[1] *This annex reproduces the sections on the short-term and medium-term economic outlook from the report of the Panel of Independent Forecasters submitted to the Chancellor of the Exchequer on 2 November 1994. The full report, which includes members' individual submissions on the economic outlook and policy, is available from HM Treasury.*

Table 3B.1 Summary of short-term forecasts

		Percentage changes on a year earlier unless otherwise stated		
		Average	Range	
			Lowest	Highest
Real GDP	1994	3·6	3·5	3·6
	1995	3·0	2·5	3·7
Unemployment (millions)	1994 Q4	2·5	2·5	2·6
	1995 Q4	2·3	1·9	2·6
RPI excluding MIPs	1994 Q4	2·2	1·9	2·3
	1995 Q4	2·9	1·9	3·9
Current account (£ billion)	1994	−4·8	−6·5	−3·4
	1995	−5·0	−12·0	2·1
PSBR (£ billion)	1994–95	34	30	36
	1995–96	25	17	32

Demand and activity

3B.5 With actual data for the first three quarters of the year already available, there is little to play for on **GDP** in 1994, and we are all forecasting growth of 3½ per cent. We all expect output to continue rising at a healthy rate next year – sufficient, for all but one of us, to result in further falls in unemployment. But we differ on how 1995 will turn out compared to 1994: three of us expect a slowdown in non-oil growth to 2½ per cent growth or less, Godley sees non-oil growth turning out much the same as in 1994, while Davies and Minford foresee an acceleration to around 3¾ per cent.

3B.6 The pessimists see recent fast growth as temporary, caused by expansionary policy measures – falling interest rates and sterling's devaluation. With the force of these measures now spent, GDP will revert to slower growth, as demand is constrained by the continuing high levels of debt, subdued asset prices, slow credit growth, and the fiscal tightening. To them the very large financial surplus run by the private sector in the first half of 1994 is evidence of retrenchment, as strong profit and income growth is channelled into debt repayment – which they expect to see continuing. But Davies, Godley and Minford think the private sector surplus will be unwound more quickly, giving stronger investment and consumption. Minford also expects continuing strong export growth.

3B.7 So our forecasts of consumption and investment generally divide into two camps in the same way as total GDP. Nevertheless we agree that over the next year the balance of growth will continue to shift away from consumption towards investment, and, for most of us, net trade.

Trade

3B.8 The balance of payments data released over the summer have been the biggest surprise since we last met. The current account deficit has been reduced to only about ½ per cent of GDP in the first half of this year, about 1 percentage point lower than in the pre-devaluation year of 1992. Arithmetically, this improvement has all been due to two factors: trade in oil and net flows on interest, profits and dividends. Although exports have risen sharply, non-oil trade is little changed. But this represents a surprisingly good performance over a period of reviving domestic demand when we would have expected to see some deterioration of the trade balance.

Table 3B.2 Forecasts of domestic demand

		Percentage changes on a year earlier		
		Average	Range	
			Lowest	Highest
Domestic demand	1994	2·9	2·7	3·5
	1995	2·9	2·1	3·7
Consumer spending	1994	2·3	2·0	2·6
	1995	2·1	1·6	2·9
Fixed investment	1994	5·1	3·4	6·8
	1995	6·3	4·6	7·7
Stockbuilding[1]	1994	0·4	0·3	0·8
	1995	0·2	0·0	0·7
Government consumption	1994	1·3	1·0	1·9
	1995	0·8	0·4	1·4

[1] *Contribution to GDP growth, per cent.*

3B.9 Even excluding oil and other "erratics", the latest figures show 10 per cent annual growth of goods **exports** in volume terms. We see the strength of exports as principally due to two factors encouraging firms to switch production towards foreign markets: the increase in export profitability following the devaluation, and the relative weakness of domestic demand. In addition, the growth of UK export markets, especially in Europe, has been considerably faster than we had anticipated. Taking on board the latest exports data leads, for most of us, to a doubling of our forecasts of export growth in 1994 since May, to around 7–8 per cent. We have all also revised up our forecasts of export growth in 1995, which now lie in the range 5¼–7 per cent.

3B.10 The latest data show a slight fall in **import** volumes. We interpret this as partly erratic and partly associated with the slower growth of domestic demand, and our forecasts of import growth are generally not greatly changed either this year or next, when they range from 4 to 7 per cent.

3B.11 Putting export and import volumes together, the data suggest that net trade will make a sizeable contribution to GDP growth in 1994, up to ¾ per cent. We expect net trade to contribute less to growth in 1995; mostly about 0–¼ per cent, though Godley expects this year's improvement to be reversed next year with a negative contribution of ½ per cent.

Table 3B.3 Forecasts of net trade and the current account

		Average	Range	
			Lowest	Highest
Exports	1994	7·8	7·1[2]	8·2
(per cent growth)	1995	6·0	5·2	7·0
Imports	1994	5·7	5·1	7·5[2]
(per cent growth)	1995	5·6	3·9	7·2[2]
Net trade[1]	1994	0·7	0·4	0·8
	1995	0·1	−0·5	0·4
Current account	1994	−4·8	−6·5	−3·4
(£ billion)	1995	−5·0	−12·0	2·1

[1] Contribution to GDP growth, per cent.
[2] Non-oil.

3B.12 The **terms of trade** (the ratio of export to import prices) fell after sterling's exit from the ERM in September 1992, and past experience led most to expect them to remain lower. But export prices subsequently rose very quickly, bringing the terms of trade back up to pre-exit levels or above by early 1993, since when they have been fairly steady — albeit falling slightly recently. Some of us interpret this experience as evidence that the UK should now be viewed as a small open economy which takes the world price rather than influencing it. In the extreme case, the economy can sell as much of its output abroad as it wants, with the balance of payments deficit simply representing the difference between domestic capacity and domestic demand. While the rest of us mostly accept that the UK is becoming more like this model, we think UK exports are still primarily determined by world demand and relative prices. In this view, the post-devaluation experience shows firms seizing the opportunity to raise profits as quickly as possible by raising prices, rather than trying to expand immediate market share, though higher export profitability may boost supply and market share over time.

3B.13 Whatever our views on the implications of the behaviour of the terms of trade, none of us expect them to change dramatically in the short term — though there is a risk of fast import price growth due to commodity price increases. So our forecasts of the visible trade deficit follow our different views on net trade volumes. Adding on invisibles, which have benefited from a very large improvement to net investment income, leads to sharp revisions to our forecasts of the 1994 **current account** deficit, which have halved since May to lie in the range £3½–6½ billion. Our forecasts for 1995 range widely, from a deficit of £12 billion to a surplus of £2 billion. This not only reflects differences of view on net trade, but also the extent to which we think the improvement to investment income will turn out to be erratic.

The labour market 3B.14 Interpretation of recent developments in the labour market is confused by the discrepancy between the two principal sources of **employment** data: the Labour Force Survey (LFS) of households and the employer-based data. The former has shown a rise of 330,000 in the recovery while the latter has yet to show any sustained upturn at all. We are strongly inclined to believe the LFS figures, which are consistent with the unemployment numbers and closer to the usual experience that participation increases during the recovery stage of the cycle. Possible reasons why the employer-based data may be under-recording employment include:

- failure to pick up employment in new businesses;
- rising employment in the construction industry, which is very cyclical but notoriously difficult to measure;
- the general switch to employing workers on short-term fixed contracts, whom firms may not regard as employees.

3B.15 The two sources of **unemployment** data, the LFS and the claimant count, are much more consistent. Both show falls of around 300,000 since the peak, and are evolving much as we expected in May. Our forecasts for the end of this year are therefore little changed since then, at close to 2½ million. Most of us project a fall of around ¼ million through 1995. However Currie forecasts slower growth to lead to unemployment rising slightly during part of next year before resuming its downward trend, while Minford forecasts a sharp fall, to below 2 million – partly because he expects strong growth and partly because he believes unemployment will revert to a much lower trend rate than experienced during the 1980s.

Monetary developments 3B.16 The monetary indicators have surprised us again. After showing signs of slowing down earlier in the year, **M0** growth has picked up again to around 6½–7 per cent since the summer, well above the Government's 0–4 per cent monitoring range. Most of us regard M0 as heavily influenced (in a somewhat unpredictable way) by the transition to a low inflation, low interest rate environment. In the light of other indicators, we are inclined to give it relatively little weight in our inflation forecasts. But Davies pays it more attention, noting that whatever its shortcomings, it has proved the best single leading indicator of inflation in the past. We expect narrow money growth to slow over the next year or so, to the region of 4 per cent.

3B.17 **M4** has followed entirely the opposite course to M0, slowing down recently after picking up earlier in the year. It would have been weaker still without the underfunding the authorities have been engaged in recently. But it is easier to be confident of the reasons for the slow growth of broad money, as it matches the slowdown in growth of consumer credit associated with the weak housing market, and low company sector borrowing. Although surprised by the developments, we are not generally concerned by the broad money figures in themselves. We mostly expect a modest rise in M4 growth in 1995, to around 5–6 per cent by the end of the year.

Inflation 3B.18 There has been little change since May in the averages of our underlying **inflation** forecasts, at 2¼ per cent at the end of 1994 and 3 per cent at the end of 1995. Although there is still a fairly large range to our forecasts for next year, we all expect inflation to remain very subdued by the standards of anything but the most recent past, and within the Government's 1–4 per cent target range. Differences between our inflation forecasts do not reflect our views on growth in the way a simple output/inflation trade-off model would suggest: if anything, there is a rough tendency for the growth pessimists also to be inflation pessimists and the growth optimists to be inflation optimists. This reflects, at least in part, the response of policy to keep inflation on target.

Table 3B.4 Inflation forecasts

		Percentage changes on a year earlier		
		Average	Range	
			Lowest	Highest
RPI excluding MIPs	1994 Q4	2·2	1·9	2·3
	1995 Q4	2·9	1·9	3·9
RPI	1994 Q4	2·5	2·0	2·7
	1995 Q4	3·4	1·8	4·6
Average earnings	1994	4·0	3·8	4·3
	1995	4·6	4·0	5·2

3B.19 Congdon and Minford are the optimists on inflation, though for different reasons. Congdon believes that a negative output gap – the degree to which output is below its trend level – will continue to exert strong downward pressure on inflation. Minford believes that supply-side improvement to the UK economy, coupled with strong competition from abroad (principally from the newly developed Asian economies), is leading to a world of permanently lower inflation.

3B.20 The rest of us accept that increased flexibility of the supply-side could have contributed to the low inflation outturns so far, as freer labour and product markets meant prices and wages responded more to slack capacity and weak demand. But in our view this would not necessarily mean that inflation would be lower in the future than previous relationships would imply. Indeed, more flexible markets might mean a greater response of prices and wages to tightening capacity and rising demand – leading to higher inflation as the economy continues to grow. However low inflation now does affect the future path of inflation as it becomes entrenched through lower expectations.

3B.21 Our average earnings forecasts are all close to 4 per cent for 1994 and 4–5 per cent in 1995, with Congdon and Minford at the lower end of the range, in line with their inflation forecasts.

Public finances

3B.22 Our forecasts of the public finances are obviously heavily influenced by the projections we make of fiscal policy. All but Minford, who thinks the response of the public finances to strong growth and low inflation will allow the Government to cut taxes significantly from next year on, project tax rates as set out in last year's Budget. Congdon, Currie, Davies and Minford all assume unchanged real spending in the Budget, implying cash spending in 1994–95 around £5 billion lower than planned in last year's Budget because prices have turned out lower than projected. Britton and Godley make their own forecasts of government expenditure based on Government plans and also attempt to anticipate future changes in them.

3B.23 We mostly expect the **PSBR** to come in reasonably close to the latest Government forecast of £36 billion this financial year. Davies and Minford foresee somewhat lower figures, reflecting their views on public expenditure. Our forecasts for 1995–96 are mostly close to each other, in the range £24–27 billion, despite differences on growth and inflation. However Godley has a significantly higher PSBR forecast, and Minford a significantly lower one.

Table 3B.5 Summary of panel members' short-term forecasts

		\multicolumn{7}{c}{Percentage changes on a year earlier unless otherwise stated}						
		Britton	Congdon	Currie	Davies	Godley	Minford	Average
GDP	1993	2·0	2·0	2·0	2·0	2·0	2·0	2·0
	1994	3·6	3·6	3·5	3·6	3·6	3·5	3·6
	1995	2·5	2·7	2·5	3·7	3·1	3·4	3·0
Domestic demand	1993	2·1	2·1	2·1	2·1	2·1	2·1	2·1
	1994	2·9	2·7	2·7	2·8	3·5	2·7	2·9
	1995	2·5	2·3	2·1	3·7	3·5	3·2	2·9
Net trade[1]	1993	0·0	0·0	0·0	0·0	0·0	0·0	0·0
	1994	0·7	0·8	0·6	0·7	0·4	0·8	0·7
	1995	0·0	0·4	0·3	0·0	−0·5	0·2	0·1
Unemployment	1993 Q4	2·8	2·8	2·8	2·8	2·8	2·8	2·8
(millions)	1994 Q4	2·5	2·6	2·5	2·5	2·6	2·5	2·5
	1995 Q4	2·3	2·4	2·6	2·2	2·5	1·9	2·3
RPI	1993 Q4	1·6	1·6	1·6	1·6	1·6	1·6	1·6
	1994 Q4	2·6	2·6	2·3	2·7	2·6[2]	2·0	2·5
	1995 Q4	4·3	2·3	3·6	4·0	4·6[2]	1·8	3·4
RPI excluding MIPs	1993 Q4	2·7	2·7	2·7	2·7	2·7	2·7	2·7
	1994 Q4	2·2	2·2	2·1	2·3	2·3[2]	1·9	2·2
	1995 Q4	3·5	2·2	3·1	2·9	3·9[2]	1·9	2·9
Short-term interest rates	1993 Q4	5·5	5·5	5·5	5·5	5·5	5·5	5·5
(per cent)	1994 Q4	5·9	5·8	5·8	5·8	5·8	5·8	5·8
	1995 Q4	7·0	6·3	7·0	7·5	7·0	5·7	6·8
Current account	1993	−10·3	−10·3	−10·3	−10·3	−10·3	−10·3	−10·3
(£ billion)	1994	−3·4	−3·7	−4·2	−5·8	−6·5	−5·0	−4·8
	1995	−4·7	2·1	−2·4	−8·3	−12·0	−4·6	−5·0
PSBR	1993–94	45·4	45·4	45·4	45·4	48·6	45·4	45·9
(£ billion)	1994–95	36·4	34·5	35·6	32·0	35·0[3]	29·7	33·9
	1995–96	26·7	23·5	27·0	24·0	32·0[3]	16·8	25·0

[1] Contribution to GDP growth, per cent.
[2] Derived from forecast of consumer price index.
[3] Derived from forecast of general government financial deficit in calendar year.

Medium-term prospects

3B.24 This section presents our views on the medium-term prospect. Our medium-term projections are summarised in Table 3B.6. This does not include input from Congdon, who thinks medium-term projections give a misleading impression of precision. Nevertheless, if appropriate policies are maintained he believes the UK could enjoy many years of stable growth and low inflation.

3B.25 We all expect continuing **GDP** growth over the medium term. However, Britton expects growth to be relatively subdued, partly reflecting the effects of monetary and fiscal tightening. The rest of us expect growth to be somewhat higher over the medium term. Continued growth is sufficient to produce further reductions in unemployment, projected to fall below 2 million by 1997 in Davies's and Minford's forecasts. However, Britton and Godley expect slower growth over the medium term to lead to a levelling off in unemployment.

3B.26 We all expect **inflation** to remain subdued over the medium term. Minford and Congdon expect inflation to remain in the bottom half of the Government's target range. The rest of us expect inflation to pick up slightly over the next few years, and Britton and Godley project a rise in inflation slightly above the top of the target range. In all but Minford's forecasts, further increases in interest rates are assumed to be needed to keep inflation within the target range. Nevertheless, the margins of error on these projections are quite large and we put more emphasis on the fact that we expect inflation to remain subdued than on the particular part of the target range in which it is likely to lie.

3B.27 Although none of us expects a significant deterioration in the **balance of payments** over the short term, Davies and Godley continue to see medium-term trends as problematic. They are not convinced that the UK's underlying trade performance has improved much in recent years, viewing the current account improvement as being due mainly to one-off special factors, and to the benefits of a successful devaluation. The rest of us do not expect the current account deficit to change markedly over the medium term. Our views on the balance of payments and its implications for policy were set out in our previous report.

3B.28 We all project a further significant fall in the **PSBR** over the medium term. All of us, except Godley, would expect the PSBR on unchanged policy to fall sufficiently that the debt to GDP ratio would stabilise by the end of the decade. Although our projections typically do not assume unchanged policies, differences in our growth forecasts account for more of the differences in our PSBR projections than do different policy assumptions. Minford is the most optimistic, expecting a PSBR of 1 per cent of GDP by 1997–98 even allowing for some tax cuts. Godley takes the most pessimistic view of the public finances: he expects large deficits to persist over the medium term, largely because the tax increases already announced are barely sufficient to compensate for the loss of revenue from North Sea oil, and thinks further restriction will eventually be needed to achieve the sustainability of the internal and external position.

Table 3B.6 Summary of panel members' medium-term forecasts

Percentage changes on a year earlier unless otherwise stated

		Britton	Currie	Davies	Godley	Minford	Average
GDP	1993	2·0	2·0	2·0	2·0	2·0	2·0
	1994	3·6	3·5	3·6	3·6	3·5	3·6
	1995	2·5	2·5	3·7	3·1	3·4	3·0
	1996	2·2	2·4	2·8	2·5	3·4	2·7
	1997	1·8	2·8	2·7	2·5	3·0	2·6
Unemployment	1993	2·9	2·9	2·9	2·9	2·9	2·9
(millions)	1994	2·6	2·6	2·6	2·6	2·6	2·6
	1995	2·4	2·5	2·3	2·5	2·2	2·4
	1996	2·3	2·5	2·1	2·4	1·6	2·2
	1997	2·3	2·4	1·8	2·4	1·2	2·0
RPI excluding MIPs	1993	3·0	3·0	3·0	3·0	3·0	3·0
	1994	2·4	2·3	2·4	2·6	2·3	2·4
	1995	3·1	2·8	2·8	3·9	1·6	2·8
	1996	3·9	3·1	3·3	4·0	1·8	3·2
	1997	4·1	3·3	3·7	4·2	2·4	3·5
Current account[1]	1993	−1·6	−1·6	−1·6	−1·6	−1·6	−1·6
	1994	−0·5	−0·6	−0·9	−1·1	−0·9	−0·8
	1995	−0·7	−0·3	−1·2	−1·6	−0·7	−0·9
	1996	−0·9	−0·2	−1·7	−2·2	−1·1	−1·2
	1997	−0·8	−0·2	−2·0	−2·9	−1·3	−1·4
PSBR[1]	1993–94	7·1	7·1	7·1	7·1	7·1	7·1
	1994–95	5·3	5·2	4·8	5·1[2]	4·3	4·9
	1995–96	3·7	3·8	3·3	4·3[2]	2·3	3·5
	1996–97	2·9	3·2	2·3	3·5[2]	2·2	2·8
	1997–98	2·8	2·7	1·3	2·9[2]	1·2	2·2

[1] *Per cent of GDP.*
[2] *Derived from forecast of general government financial deficit in calendar year.*

4 The public finances

4.01 This chapter sets out projections for the public finances up to 1999–2000 after allowing for the measures in the Budget and the new assessment of economic prospects. It also includes an analysis of changes from the November 1993 Budget projections. Historical series and further detail on the forecasts for 1994–95 and 1995–96 are presented in Annex A. Annex B provides a guide to the different accounting conventions used in presentation of the public finances in this chapter and elsewhere.

4.02 The main projections suggest that the public sector borrowing requirement (PSBR) is likely to return more quickly to balance than envisaged a year ago, with the public sector current account in surplus by 1997–98. Before then, the deficit will have fallen below the reference level of 3 per cent for the European Union's excessive deficits procedure.

The budget deficit

4.03 The projected path for the PSBR is summarised in Table 4.1.

Table 4.1 Public sector borrowing requirement[1]

	Outturn	Forecast		Projection[2]			
	1993–94	1994–95	1995–96	1996–97	1997–98	1998–99	1999–2000
£ billion							
General government expenditure	277·5	288·9	302·0	313	323	332	342
General government receipts	230·8	252·5	278·9	298	316	332	349
General government borrowing requirement	46·7	36·5	23·1	15	7	0	−8
PCMOB[3]	−1·3	−2·0	−1·6	−2	−2	−1	−1
PSBR	**45·4**	**34·4**	**21·5**	**13**	**5**	**−1**	**−9**
Per cent of money GDP							
General government expenditure	43½	42½	42	41¼	40¾	39¾	39
General government receipts	36	37¼	38¾	39¼	39¾	39¾	40
General government borrowing requirement	7¼	5½	3¼	2	1	0	−1
PCMOB[3]	−¼	−¼	−¼	−¼	−¼	0	0
PSBR	**7**	**5**	**3**	**1¾**	**¾**	**0**	**−1**
Money GDP – £ billion	639	678	720	758	796	834	873

[1] In this and other tables, constituent items may not sum to totals because of rounding.
[2] Projections are rounded to the nearest £1 billion from 1996–97 onwards.
[3] Public corporations' market and overseas borrowing.

4 The public finances

The PSBR in the short term

4.04 The outturn for the PSBR in 1993–94 was £45·4 billion, 7 per cent of GDP. This was a cyclical peak in borrowing, which is now running at a significantly lower level. The latest forecast for the PSBR in 1994–95 is £34½ billion, 5 per cent of GDP.

4.05 Taking into account the tax changes announced in the Budget and the new public expenditure plans, the PSBR in 1995–96 is forecast to fall to £21½ billion, 3 per cent of GDP. This means that the PSBR will have more than halved in two years.

4.06 Receipts in 1995–96 are forecast to rise substantially faster than money GDP, reflecting the phased tax increases announced in the two 1993 Budgets and a cyclical recovery in corporation tax receipts. Public expenditure is projected to grow more slowly than GDP despite rising debt interest payments.

Medium-term PSBR projections

4.07 The projections of the public finances in the medium term are based on the assumptions for the economy set out in Annex A to Chapter 3. As the economic recovery continues and the measures in the 1993 and 1994 Budgets come through, the PSBR falls further, with a small debt repayment projected by 1998–99. Receipts rise slightly faster than GDP, and public expenditure is projected to fall as a percent of GDP in line with the new spending plans.

Other measures of the fiscal stance

4.08 Table 4.2, which is the cash counterpart of Table 1.1, sets out projections of the current deficit of the public sector and the financial deficit for both general government and the public sector as a whole, and shows how they relate to the PSBR. The deficit on the public sector's current account is forecast to fall steadily from £28 billion in 1994–95, and give way to a surplus from 1997–98 onwards.

4.09 Net capital spending – the public sector's balance on capital account – is forecast at £12½ billion in 1994–95, when it is boosted by temporarily high local authorities' spending. Slightly lower net spending is projected for future years. The public sector financial deficit (PSFD) is projected to fall steadily from £40½ billion in 1994–95, with a surplus achieved by the end of the decade. The gap between the PSFD and the PSBR falls from around £6 billion in 1994–95 as privatisation proceeds decline.

4 The public finances

4.10 The general government financial deficit (GGFD) – the measure used to monitor budget deficits under the European Union excessive deficits procedure – is forecast at £42 billion for 1994–95, 6¼ per cent of GDP. It is forecast to fall to 2¼ per cent of GDP in 1996–97, below the 3 per cent reference level for deficits used in the excessive deficits procedure. The GGFD is slightly higher than the PSFD up to 1997–98 because public corporations are forecast to be in small financial surplus.

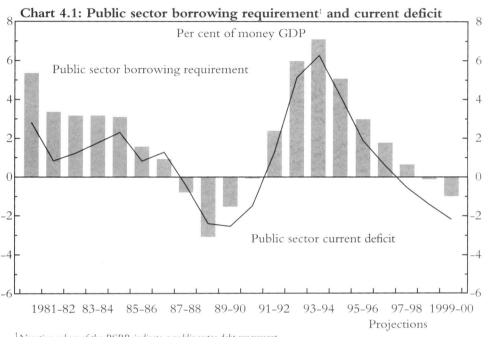

Chart 4.1: Public sector borrowing requirement[1] and current deficit

[1] Negative values of the PSBR indicate a public sector debt repayment.

Table 4.2 The public sector's finances

	£ billion						
	Outturn	Forecast		Projection[4]			
	1993–94	1994–95	1995–96	1996–97	1997–98	1998–99	1999–2000
Receipts[1]	231.9	256.4	282.7	302	319	335	352
Current expenditure[1, 2]	272.0	284.4	296.2	306	314	323	333
Current balance[1]	**−40·0**	**−28·0**	**−13·5**	**−4**	**4**	**12**	**19**
Net capital spending[1, 3]	11.4	12.4	11.6	11	11	11	11
Financial deficit[1]	**51·4**	**40·4**	**25·2**	**16**	**6**	**−1**	**−8**
Privatisation proceeds and other financial transactions	6.1	5.9	3.6	2	1	0	1
PSBR	**45·4**	**34·4**	**21·5**	**13**	**5**	**−1**	**−9**
General government financial deficit – £ billion	50.9	41.9	26.1	17	7	−1	−9
– per cent of GDP	8	6¼	3¾	2¼	1	−¼	−1

[1] Figures on a national accounts basis. See Annex B.
[2] Includes depreciation of fixed capital.
[3] Net of depreciation and less capital transfer receipts.
[4] Rounded to the nearest £1 billion.

4 The public finances

Public sector debt

4.11 Table 4.3 sets out projections for the stock of net public sector debt and gross general government debt. (Definitions are set out in Annex B.) Net public sector debt at end-March 1994 stood at £252 billion, 38¼ per cent of GDP. The latest forecasts for the PSBR imply a further increase in the ratio, which reaches a peak of 42¾ per cent of GDP at end-March 1996. Thereafter the ratio is projected to fall steadily as the PSBR is brought down further.

Table 4.3 Public sector debt[1]

	Outturn	Forecast		Projection			
	1993–94	1994–95	1995–96	1996–97	1997–98	1998–99	1999–2000
Net public sector debt							
£ billion[2]	252	285	316	329	335	335	327
per cent of GDP[3]	38¼	40¾	42¾	42¼	41¼	39¼	36¾
Gross general government debt							
£ billion[2]	310	334	364	379	388	389	383
per cent of GDP[3]	47	48	49¼	48¾	47½	45½	43

[1] At end-March.
[2] Rounded to the nearest £1 billion.
[3] GDP centred on end-March. Ratios for excessive deficits procedure use GDP for year ending in March, which raises ratio by around 1¼ per cent.

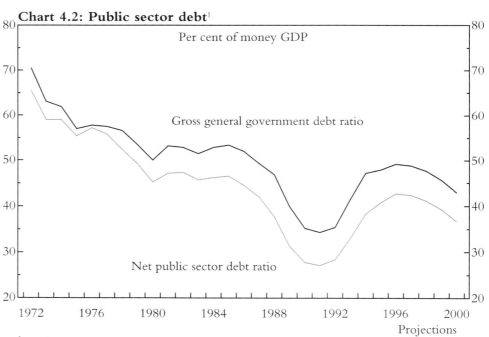

Chart 4.2: Public sector debt[1]

[1] At end-March as a percent of money GDP in four quarters centred on end-March, (see footnote 3 to Table 4.3).

4.12 Gross general government debt, the measure used for the European Union's excessive deficits procedure, stood at 47 per cent of GDP at end-March 1994. It is projected to peak at 49¼ per cent of GDP at end-March 1996, comfortably below the reference level of 60 per cent, and to fall back thereafter.

4 The public finances

General government receipts

4.13 Table 4.4 shows the outturns for 1993–94, short-term forecasts for 1994–95 and 1995–96 and medium-term projections up to 1999–2000 for general government receipts and its principal components. Table 4A.1 gives a more detailed breakdown for the 1993–94 outturns and for the short-term forecasts.

Table 4.4 General government receipts

	£ billion						
	Outturn	Forecast		Projection[3]			
	1993–94	1994–95	1995–96	1996–97	1997–98	1998–99	1999–2000
Income tax	58·4	64·2	70·1	75	79	85	90
Corporation tax	14·9	20·1	26·4	31	34	36	38
Value added tax	38·9	43·3	49·0	53	56	58	61
Excise duties[1]	24·2	26·3	28·0	30	33	35	38
Other taxes and royalties[2]	38·6	39·7	43·0	46	48	48	49
Social security contributions	38·7	42·5	44·5	47	49	52	54
Other receipts	17·1	16·3	17·8	17	18	18	19
General government receipts	**230·8**	**252·5**	**278·9**	**298**	**316**	**332**	**349**
GGR/GDP ratio – per cent	36	37¼	38¾	39¼	39¾	39¾	40

[1] *Fuel, alcohol and tobacco duties.*
[2] *Includes council tax as well as other central government taxes.*
[3] *Rounded to the nearest £1 billion.*

Receipts in 1994–95

4.14 General government receipts are now expected to rise by 9½ per cent in 1994–95, well above the forecast increase in money GDP. This will be the first time for five years that receipts have risen faster than GDP. Much of the rise reflects the effects of tax increases announced in the two 1993 Budgets. But corporation tax receipts are also forecast to rise sharply – by around 35 per cent – because of the cyclical recovery in profits last year.

Receipts in 1995–96 and beyond

4.15 General government receipts are forecast to rise by 10½ per cent in 1995–96, again much faster than money GDP as the cyclical recovery continues. The further changes in income tax reliefs and VAT announced in the two 1993 Budgets, and due to take effect in April 1995, will raise taxes by a further £2¾ billion in 1995–96 and another £¾ billion in 1996–97. The tax changes announced in this Budget do not change the projections significantly. Leaving aside the temporary reduction in business rates from the new transitional relief scheme they reduce taxes by around £½ billion a year.

4.16 After 1996–97, when the tax increases have worked fully through, receipts are projected to increase at an average 5½ per cent per annum, marginally higher than money GDP reflecting the over-indexation of tobacco and road fuel duties and real fiscal drag.

4 The public finances

Taxes as a share of GDP

4.17 Tax and social security revenues fell quite markedly as a share of GDP during the recession to reach a trough of 33¾ per cent in 1993–94, the lowest level for 20 years. But following the tax increases announced in the two 1993 Budgets, and with a strong cyclical recovery now under way, the tax/GDP ratio is expected to rise sharply in 1994–95 to 35¼ per cent, 1½ percentage points up on the previous year.

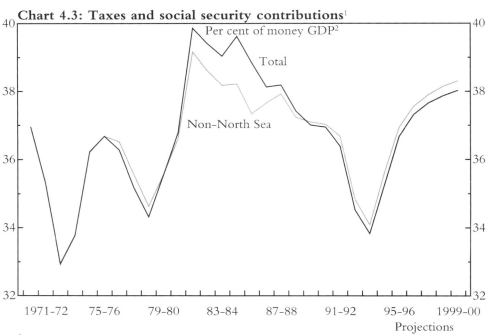

Chart 4.3: Taxes and social security contributions[1]

[1] On a national accounts accruals basis, includes local authority taxes.
[2] Non-North Sea taxes and social security contributions are expressed as a percent of non-North Sea money GDP.

4.18 The same factors contribute to a further sharp rise in the tax/GDP ratio forecast for 1995–96, which will bring the ratio back close to the level at the beginning of the recession. Thereafter, on the conventional assumption of no changes in tax rates and an indexed tax system (except where a policy of real rises in rates has been announced), the ratio is projected to continue rising, but at a much slower rate.

General government expenditure

4.19 The Government's objective for public spending is to reduce general government expenditure (GGE) excluding privatisation proceeds as a share of GDP over time. This aggregate includes spending within the Control Total, cyclical social security expenditure, debt interest payments and various accounting adjustments needed for consistency with the national accounts. The new plans show real GGE growth over the next three years averaging between ½ and ¾ per cent per annum, well below the projected growth rate of the economy.

4.20 Table 4.5 shows the 1993–94 outturn, forecasts for 1994–95 and projections up to 1999–2000 for GGE and its main components. The projections up to 1997–98 are consistent with the new public spending plans. Figures for the later years assume that Control Total spending will grow by 1 per cent a year in real terms.

Table 4.5 General government expenditure

	£ billion						
	Outturn	Forecast		Projection[1]			
	1993–94	1994–95	1995–96	1996–97	1997–98	1998–99	1999–2000
Control Total	241·4	249·6	255·7	263	272	280	289
Cyclical social security	14·3	14·1	14·1	14	14	15	15
Central government debt interest	19·2	22·1	24·5	26	26	26	26
Privatisation proceeds	−5·4	−6·3	−3·0	−3	−2	−1	−1
Accounting adjustments	8·0	9·5	10·7	13	13	12	12
GGE	**277·5**	**288·9**	**302·0**	**313**	**323**	**332**	**342**
GGE[2]/GDP ratio – per cent	44¼	43½	42½	41¾	41	40	39¼
Real growth – per cent:							
Control Total	1¼	1¼	−¾	½	1	1	1
GGE[2]	2¼	2¼	0	1	¾	½	¾

[1] *Rounded to the nearest £1 billion.*
[2] *Excluding privatisation proceeds.*

Expenditure in 1994–95

4.21 GGE excluding privatisation proceeds in 1994–95 is now forecast to rise by 4¼ per cent, a bit below the expected growth in money GDP. Control Total spending is forecast at £249½ billion, £1¼ billion lower than the plans in last year's Budget. This still represents a real terms increase of 1¼ per cent on 1993–94 spending.

Expenditure over the medium term

4.22 The new public spending plans provide for Control Total spending to rise at under 3 per cent a year in cash terms over the next three years. This represents an average of only ¼ per cent a year growth in real terms. The projected increase in GGE is a little higher – an average of 3¼ per cent per annum in cash, or between ½ and ¾ per cent in real terms.

4.23 Outside the Control Total, cyclical social security is broadly flat in cash terms, as Budget measures offset the underlying upward trend. However accounting adjustments are projected to rise, reflecting among other things the spending of National Lottery proceeds. Debt interest payments are also rising, as a consequence of the recent high borrowing requirements. Central government debt interest is forecast to increase by over one-third in the three years from 1993–94 to 1996–97; thereafter it is projected to flatten out as borrowing is reduced.

4 The public finances

Expenditure as a share of GDP

4.24 The ratio of GGE (excluding privatisation proceeds) to GDP, which increased sharply during the recession, stood at 44¼ per cent in 1993–94, marginally below its peak in the previous year. The ratio is expected to fall by around ¾ percentage point in 1994–95, and the new public expenditure plans imply a further fall of around 2½ percentage points over the next three years. The medium-term projections show this fall continuing, with the GGE/GDP ratio in 1999–2000 down to 39¼ per cent, a similar level to 1988–89.

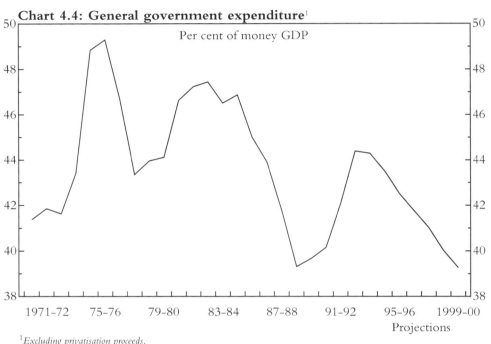

Chart 4.4: General government expenditure[1]

[1] Excluding privatisation proceeds.

Changes since the last Budget

4.25 Table 4.6 summarises changes in the PSBR projections since the last Budget. More detail for 1994–95 and 1995–96 is given in Annex A.

Table 4.6 Changes since the last Budget[1]

	£ billion					
	Outturn	Forecast[2]		Projection[2]		
	1993–94	1994–95	1995–96	1996–97	1997–98	1998–99
General government expenditure[3]	−3·1	−2·1	−8	−9	−11	−13
Privatisation proceeds[4]	−0·1	−0·8	−2	−2	−1	0
General government receipts	+1·1	0·0	−1½	−3	−5½	−8½
Public corporations' market and overseas borrowing	+0·5	−0·1	+½	+½	0	+1½
PSBR	**−3·7**	**−3·0**	**−8½**	**−7½**	**−6**	**−3**

[1] November 1993 forecast adjusted for classification changes.
[2] Rounded to the nearest £½ billion from 1995–96.
[3] Excluding privatisation proceeds.
[4] A minus sign indicates higher privatisation proceeds.

4 The public finances

PSBR in 1993–94 and 1994–95

4.26 The outturn for the PSBR in 1993–94 was £3·7 billion lower than the forecast made in the last Budget, adjusted for subsequent classification changes. The forecast for 1994–95 has been reduced by £3 billion. In both cases this is due primarily to lower cash spending.

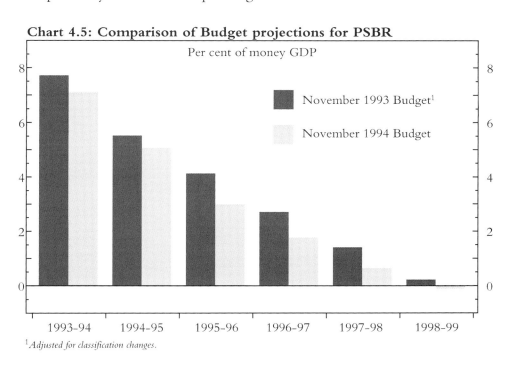

Chart 4.5: Comparison of Budget projections for PSBR

[1] Adjusted for classification changes.

The projections

4.27 The PSBR projections are lower than those in the last Budget. Spending is lower throughout in cash terms reflecting the new plans in the Budget. In the short run, apart from the impact of the Budget measures, receipts are little changed because the impact of lower prices is offset by higher activity. But in the medium term receipts are lower. The Budget measures contribute relatively little to these lower medium-term receipts, as Table 4.7 shows. General government receipts are little different as a percent of GDP from the projections in the last Budget.

Table 4.7 Changes in the projection of receipts[1]

	£ billion			
	1995–96	1996–97	1997–98	1998–99
Current prices				
Budget measures to tax/NICs[2]	−1	−½	−½	−½
Other changes to tax/NICs[3]	−½	−2	−5	−8
Changes to other receipts	+½	−½	0	−½
Total change in GGR	**−1½**	**−3**	**−5½**	**−8½**
1993–94 prices				
Total change in GGR	**+5**	**+3½**	**+2**	**−½**
Change in GGR/GDP ratio – per cent	0	0	−¼	−½

[1] Rounded to the nearest £½ billion.
[2] Changes from indexed base. See Table 1.4.
[3] Mainly resulting from changes in inflation and growth projections.

4.28 Most of the reduction in general government expenditure is accounted for by the reductions in Control Total spending announced in the Budget. But there are also significant reductions in cyclical social security, both because prices and unemployment are lower than envisaged a year ago and because of the measures in the Budget. The projection of debt interest is little changed from a year ago; the impact of higher long-term interest rates is offset by the effect of a lower borrowing profile.

Table 4.8 Changes in the public spending projections[1]

	£ billion			
	1995–96	1996–97	1997–98	1998–99
Current prices				
Control Total	−7	−8½	−9	−9
Cyclical social security[2]	−1½	−2	−2½	−3
Debt interest	0	+½	−½	−½
Accounting adjustments	0	+1	+1	−½
Privatisation proceeds[4]	−2	−2	−1	0
Total change in GGE	**−10**	**−11**	**−12**	**−13**
1993-94 prices				
Control Total	−½	−1½	−2	−2
Cyclical social security[2]	−1	−1½	−2	−2
Debt interest	+½	+1	+½	0
Accounting adjustments	+½	+1	+1	0
Privatisation proceeds[4]	−2	−2	−1	0
Total change in GGE	**−2½**	**−3**	**−3½**	**−4**
Change in GGE[3]/GDP ratio – per cent	−¾	−¾	−¾	−1

[1] Rounded to the nearest £½ billion.
[2] Of which Budget measures:

−Current prices	−0.4	−0.7	−0.9	−1
−1993–94 prices	−0.3	−0.6	−0.8	−1

[3] Excluding privatisation proceeds.
[4] A minus sign indicates higher privatisation proceeds.

4.29 The level of prices (as measured by the GDP deflator) now forecast for 1995-96 is 2½ per cent lower than assumed in last year's Budget projections, and this reduction is projected to persist in the medium term. The cash reductions announced in the Budget bring Control Total spending in real terms below the levels in last year's Budget plans, as Table 4.8 illustrates. On top of this, the cash reductions in cyclical social security represent a significant real terms reduction in spending. As a result, the GGE/GDP ratio is lower throughout than in last year's Budget projections.

Funding policy

4.30 Funding policy will continue on the basis set out in the 1994–95 MTFS and the gilts remit published on 17 March 1994 and updated in the Summer Economic Forecast. Table 4.9 updates the funding arithmetic to allow for the new PSBR forecast, the latest information on gilts sales, National Savings and other changes. It is expected that £10·5 billion of gilt sales will be required in the months November 1994 to March 1995 to achieve full funding.

4.31 New remits for gilts and National Savings will be published just before the start of the financial year 1995–96. The remits will explain funding policy in more detail and how it will be implemented.

Table 4.9 Funding requirement forecast for 1994–95

	£ billion
PSBR	34·4
Gilts maturing	8·5
Less Cumulative overfund and gilts sales to monetary sector in 1992–93	10·2
Funding requirement	32·7
Less Net National Savings inflow	3·5
Gilts sales required for full funding	29·2
Less Gilts sales (April – October 1994)	18·7
Further gilts sales required (November – March 1994–95) for full funding	10·5

Margins of error and alternative projections

Average errors   **4.32** The PSBR forecasts are subject to a wide margin of error. Over the past ten years the average absolute error on forecasts of the current year made in the autumn (November Budget forecast for last year, Autumn Statement forecasts for previous years) has averaged ¾ per cent of GDP, equivalent to plus or minus £4½ billion in today's terms. The average absolute error in projections for the year ahead, adjusted for subsequent Budget measures, is 1½ per cent of GDP, or plus or minus £10½ billion in today's terms.

Alternative projections

4.33 There are inevitably uncertainties about the path of the economy and these can be a source of error in the medium-term projections for the public finances. Cyclical variations in output automatically produce variations in tax revenues and, to a lesser extent, in government expenditure. Given a higher degree of spare capacity, growth could be stronger for a period without generating inflationary pressures. On the other hand some indicators suggest rather little spare capacity, in which case sustainable medium-term growth might be weaker. The growth rates in Table 4.10 differ from the main projection by ½ per cent in either direction from 1995–96.

Table 4.10 Variant growth projections[1]

	1995–96	1996–97	1997–98	1998–99	1999–2000
Higher growth	3½	3¼	3¼	3¼	3¼
Lower growth	2½	2¼	2¼	2¼	2¼

[1] *Non-oil GDP.*

4.34 Table 4.11 shows the path of the PSBR on unchanged policies in these alternative projections. Public expenditure within the Control Total is assumed to be unchanged, but cyclical social security and debt interest payments are allowed to vary. Tax rates, allowances and thresholds are assumed to be at the same levels as in the main projection, with revenues allowed to vary automatically with the output path.

Table 4.11 Variant PSBR projections

	Per cent of GDP				
	1995–96	1996–97	1997–98	1998–99	1999–2000
Higher growth	2¾	1¼	–¼	–1¼	–2½
Lower growth	3	2¼	1½	1¼	½

4.35 The stronger growth projection moves the public sector into significant surplus by the end of the decade on present plans. Even in the slower growth projection, public expenditure restraint is sufficient to keep the PSBR on a downward trend.

Annex A to Chapter 4
Further analyses of the public finances

4A.1 This Annex contains a number of further analyses of the forecasts of the public finances in 1994–95 and 1995–96. There are also two tables which set out historical series for the PSBR and its main components, including general government expenditure (GGE), excluding privatisation proceeds, and general government receipts.

4A.2 The following analyses are included:

(i) **General government receipts** – further tax-by-tax details of the forecasts for 1994–95 and 1995–96 (Table 4A.1);

(ii) **Sectoral breakdown of PSBR** forecasts for 1994–95 (Table 4A.2);

(iii) **Central government transactions on a cash basis** – forecasts for 1994–95 and 1995–96 (Table 4A.3);

(iv) **Economic category analyses of local authority and public corporations transactions** (Tables 4A.4 and 4A.5);

(v) **A full analysis of receipts and expenditure by economic category** for 1994–95 and 1995–96 (Table 4A.6);

(vi) **Changes to PSBR forecasts** for 1994–95 and 1995–96 since the last Budget and since the Summer Economic Forecast (Table 4A.7);

(vii) **Historical series for the PSBR and its main components** (Tables 4A.8 and 4A.9).

General government receipts

Table 4A.1 General government receipts[1]

	£ billion			
	1993–94	1994–95		1995–96
	Outturn	Last Budget forecast	Latest forecast	Forecast
Inland Revenue				
Income tax	58·4	64·4	64·2	70·1
Corporation tax[2]	14·9	17·6	20·1	26·4
Petroleum revenue tax	0·4	1·0	0·7	0·7
Capital gains tax	0·7	1·3	0·8	0·8
Inheritance tax	1·3	1·4	1·4	1·5
Stamp duties	1·7	1·8	1·8	2·0
Total Inland Revenue	**77·5**	**87·5**	**89·1**	**101·5**
Customs and Excise				
Value added tax	38·9	43·1	43·3	49·0
Fuel duties	12·5	14·5	14·2	15·6
Tobacco duties	6·5	7·2	6·8	7·0
Spirits duties	1·7	1·8	1·7	1·7
Wine duties	1·1	1·1	1·1	1·2
Beer and cider duties	2·4	2·6	2·6	2·6
Betting and gaming duties	1·1	1·2	1·2	1·2
Customs duties	2·0	2·0	2·0	2·1
Agricultural levies	0·2	0·1	0·2	0·2
Air passenger duty	0·0	0·1	0·1	0·3
Insurance premium tax	0·0	0·3	0·2	0·7
Total Customs and Excise	**66·3**	**73·9**	**73·2**	**81·5**
Vehicle excise duties	3·6	3·8	3·8	4·0
Oil royalties	0·6	0·6	0·5	0·5
Business rates[3]	12·6	13·0	12·3	13·8
Other taxes and royalties	5·8	5·9	5·9	5·8
Total taxes and royalty receipts	**166·4**	**184·8**	**184·9**	**207·2**
Social security contributions	38·7	42·8	42·5	44·5
Council tax	8·6	8·6	8·8	9·2
Interest and dividends	5·1	5·4	4·2	4·6
Gross trading surpluses and rent	5·1	4·3	5·2	5·7
Other receipts[4]	6·9	6·4	6·9	7·6
General government receipts	**230·8**	**252·4**	**252·5**	**278·9**
North Sea revenues[5]	1·2	2·1	1·6	2·2

[1] On a cash basis. See Annex B.
[2] Includes advance corporation tax (net of repayments): 7·8 7·4 7·6 8·6
(also includes North Sea corporation tax after ACT set-off, and corporation tax on gains).
[3] Includes district council rates in Northern Ireland.
[4] Includes accruals adjustments for index-linked gilts.
[5] North Sea corporation tax (before ACT set-off), petroleum revenue tax and oil royalties.

Borrowing by sector

4A.3 Central government borrowing on its own account (ie excluding borrowing for on-lending to local authorities and public corporations) more than accounted for the total PSBR in 1993–94 and is expected to do so again in 1994–95. Central government borrowing on own account in the first seven months of 1994–95 was £7·0 billion lower than in the same period of 1993–94. The forecast for 1994–95 as a whole implies borrowing in November to March which is £4½ billion lower than in the same period last year.

Table 4A.2 Public sector borrowing requirement by sector

	£ billion					
	1993–94			1994–95		
	Outturn			Outturn	Forecast	
	Apr-Oct	Nov-Mar	Total	Apr-Oct	Nov-Mar	Total
CGBR(O)[1]	28·4	19·6	48·0	21·5	15·1	36·5
LABR[2]	−1·8	−1·0	−2·8	−0·8	0·3	−0·4
PCBR[3]	−0·2	0·4	0·2	−1·5	−0·1	−1·7
PSBR	**26·4**	**19·0**	**45·4**	**19·2**	**15·3**	**34·4**

[1] *Central government borrowing requirement on own account.*
[2] *Local authority borrowing requirement.*
[3] *Public corporations' borrowing requirement.*

4A.4 Local authorities made a net repayment of £2·8 billion in 1993–94, but a smaller repayment is forecast for 1994–95. Public corporations' borrowing was £0·2 billion in 1993–94; the forecast for 1994–95 is for a repayment of £1¾ billion.

Central government transactions on a cash basis

4A.5 The monthly outturn figures for central government borrowing are measured from the cash flows into and out of central government's funds and accounts, after consolidation. Table 4A.3 sets out the 1993–94 outturn and 1994–95 and 1995–96 forecasts for central government borrowing in terms of this cash flow presentation.

Table 4A.3 Central government transactions on a cash receipts and outlays basis

	£ billion			
	1993–94	1994–95		1995–96
	Outturn	Last Budget forecast	Latest forecast	Forecast
Receipts				
Inland Revenue[1]	77·3	87·5	89·1	101·5
Customs and Excise[1]	66·9	74·2	73·4	81·7
Social security contributions (GB)	37·0	41·3	41·0	43·0
Interest and dividends	9·3	9·0	7·6	7·8
Other	18·7	17·8	17·6	18·8
Total receipts	**209·2**	**229·8**	**228·6**	**252·8**
Outlays				
Interest payments	18·8	21·6	21·4	23·0
Privatisation proceeds	−5·4	−5·5	−6·3	−3·0
Net department outlays	243·8	250·2[2]	250·0	255·6[2]
Total outlays	**257·2**	**266·3**[2]	**265·1**	**275·6**[2]
Net own account borrowing[3]	**48·0**	[4]	**36·5**	[4]

[1] *Payments to the Consolidated Fund.*
[2] *Excluding any allocation from the Reserve.*
[3] *Excludes net lending to local authorities and public corporations.*
[4] *No comparable estimate because Reserve not allocated across sectors.*

Public finances by economic category

4A.6 Table 4A.6 shows a full analysis of receipts and expenditure by economic category, with a breakdown between central government, local authorities and public corporations. Annex B explains the conventions used, which follow in most respects those in the UK national income and expenditure accounts.

4A.7 The table makes the assumption that the Reserve for 1995–96 is spent entirely on transactions that fall above the financial deficit line, although in practice allocations from the Reserve can also affect financial transactions. The Reserve for 1995–96 has been further apportioned between current and capital expenditure, on the basis of the experience of past outturns. A working assumption has been made that all of the Reserve will be spent by general government, in order to produce the projections of the general government financial deficit (GGFD) shown in Table 4.2, and the gross general government debt projections in Table 4.3. There is, however, no apportionment of the Reserve in Table 4A.6 between central government and local authorities.

4A.8 Tables 4A.4 and 4A.5 summarise the information on local authorities and public corporations transactions in Table 4A.6, and also provide outturn figures for 1993–94.

Table 4A.4 Local authority transactions

	£ billion		
	Outturn	Forecast	
	1993-94	1994-95	1995-96
Receipts			
Council tax[1]	8·1	8·6	9·2
Current grants from central government	54·7	56·4	57·6
Other current receipts[2]	7·7	8·0	8·3
Capital grants from central government	3·3	2·9	3·3
Total receipts	**73·8**	**75·9**	**78·5**
Expenditure			
Current expenditure on goods and services	49·7	50·8	52·0
Current grants and subsidies	12·7	13·9	14·8
Interest	4·4	4·3	4·4
Capital expenditure before depreciation	6·5	8·0	6·9
Total expenditure	**73·3**	**77·1**	**78·1**[3]
Financial deficit	**−0·5**	**1·2**	[4]
Net financial transactions	−2·3	−1·6	−1·3
Net borrowing	**−2·8**	**−0·4**	[4]

[1] Net of rebates and council tax benefit. Includes district council rates in Northern Ireland shown in "Taxes on expenditure" in Table 4A.6 (line 2).
[2] Includes interest receipts, rent and gross trading surplus.
[3] Excluding any allocation from the Reserve.
[4] No forecast shown because Reserve not allocated between central government and local authorities.

Table 4A.5 Public corporations' transactions

	£ billion		
	Outturn	Forecast	
	1993-94	1994-95	1995-96
Receipts			
Gross trading surplus (including subsidies)	3·2	5·4	5·4
Other current grants	0·7	0·7	0·7
Capital grants from general government	3·1	3·4	3·2
Total receipts	**7·0**	**9·5**	**9·4**
Expenditure			
Interest, dividends and taxes on income	2·3	2·2	2·2
Capital expenditure before depreciation	5·3	5·8	6·2
Total expenditure	**7·6**	**8·0**	**8·4**[1]
Financial deficit	**0·6**	**−1·5**	**−1·0**
Net financial transactions	−0·3	−0·2	−1·7
Net borrowing	**0·2**	**−1·7**	**−2·7**

[1] Assumes no allocation from the Reserve.

Table 4A.6 Public sector transactions by sub-sector and economic category

£ billion
1994–95

	Line[1]	General government — Central government	General government — Local authorities	General government — Total	Public corporations	Public sector
Current receipts[2]						
Taxes on income and royalties	1	86·2	0·0	86·2	−0·2	86·0
Taxes on expenditure	2	98·8	0·1	98·9	0·0	98·9
Taxes on capital	3	2·7	0·0	2·7	0·0	2·7
Social security contributions	4	42·8	0·0	42·8	0·0	42·8
Council tax	5	0·0	8·5	8·5	0·0	8·5
Gross trading surplus	6	−0·3	0·8	0·6	5·4	6·0
Rent and miscellaneous current transfers	7	1·0	4·4	5·4	0·6	6·0
Interest and dividends from private sector and abroad	8	1·7	0·5	2·2	0·2	2·4
Interest and dividends within public sector	9	5·8	−3·8	2·0	−2·0	0·0
Imputed charge for non-trading capital consumption	10	1·2	2·0	3·1	0·0	3·1
Total current receipts	**11**	**240·0**	**12·5**	**252·5**	**3·9**	**256·4**
Current expenditure[2]						
Current expenditure on goods and services	12	94·8	50·8	145·6	0·0	145·6
Depreciation	13	1·6	4·7	6·3	4·0	10·3
Subsidies	14	7·1	0·8	7·9	0·0	7·9
Current grants to personal sector	15	79·4	13·2	92·5	0·0	92·5
Current grants abroad	16	5·5	0·0	5·5	0·0	5·5
Current grants within public sector	17	56·4	−56·4	0·0	0·0	0·0
Debt interest	18	22·1	0·5[3]	22·6	0·0	22·6
Apportionment of Reserve	19					
Total current expenditure	**20**	**266·9**	**13·6**	**280·4**	**3·9**	**284·4**
Current deficit	**21**	**26·9**	**1·1**	**28·0**	**0·0**	**28·0**
Capital transfers	**22**	**0·0**	**0·3**	**0·3**	**−0·1**	**0·2**
Capital expenditure[2]						
Gross domestic fixed capital formation	23	5·7	6·7	12·4	5·4	17·8
Less Depreciation	24	−1·6	−4·7	−6·3	−4·0	−10·3
Increase in stocks	25	−0·1	0·0	−0·1	0·0	−0·1
Capital grants to private sector	26	3·6	1·3	4·9	0·4	5·3
Capital grants to public sector	27	6·3	−2·9	3·4	−3·4	0·0
Apportionment of Reserve	28					
Total capital expenditure	**29**	**13·8**	**0·4**	**14·2**	**−1·5**	**12·6**
Financial deficit	**30**	**40·7**	**1·2**	**41·9**	**−1·5**	**40·4**
Financial transactions						
Net lending to private sector and abroad	31	0·6	−0·3	0·2	0·0	0·2
Cash expenditure on company securities (including privatisation proceeds)	32	−6·3	0·0	−6·3	0·0	−6·3
Transactions concerning certain public sector pension schemes	33	0·7	0·0	0·7	0·0	0·7
Accruals adjustments on receipts	34	3·5	−0·6	2·9	0·0	2·9
Other accruals adjustments	35	−0·7	0·1	−0·6	0·0	−0·6
Miscellaneous financial transactions	36	−2·0	−0·8	−2·8	−0·1	−2·9
Borrowing requirement	**37**	**36·5**[4]	**−0·4**	**36·1**[4]	**−1·7**	**34·4**

[1] Current deficit (line 21) = current expenditure (line 20) − current receipts (line 11).
Financial deficit (line 30) = current deficit (line 21) − capital receipts (line 22) + capital expenditure (line 29).
Borrowing requirement (line 37) = financial deficit (line 30) + financial transactions (lines 31 to 36).

[2] On an accruals basis.

[3] Excluding local authorities' payments to central government and public corporations' payments to general government, which are in line 9.

[4] Own account borrowing requirement.

Table 4A.6 Public sector transactions by sub-sector and economic category – *continued*

£ billion

1995–96

Line[1]	General government —Central government	General government —Local authorities	General government —Total	Public corporations	Public sector	
						Current receipts[2]
1	98·1	0·0	98·1	−0·2	97·9	Taxes on income and royalties
2	108·8	0·1	108·9	0·0	108·9	Taxes on expenditure
3	3·1	0·0	3·1	0·0	3·1	Taxes on capital
4	44·8	0·0	44·8	0·0	44·8	Social security contributions
5	0·0	9·1	9·1	0·0	9·1	Council tax
6	−0·1	0·9	0·8	5·4	6·2	Gross trading surplus
7	1·6	4·6	6·2	0·6	6·8	Rent and miscellaneous current transfers
8	2·0	0·6	2·6	0·2	2·8	Interest and dividends from private sector and abroad
9	5·8	−3·7	2·0	−2·0	0·0	Interest and dividends within public sector
10	1·2	2·0	3·2	0·0	3·2	Imputed charge for non-trading capital consumption
11	**265·2**	**13·6**	**278·8**	**3·9**	**282·7**	**Total current receipts**
						Current expenditure[2]
12	96·4	52·0	148·5	0·0	148·5	Current expenditure on goods and services
13	1·6	4·9	6·5	3·8	10·3	Depreciation
14	7·3	0·8	8·1	0·0	8·1	Subsidies
15	81·2	14·0	95·2	0·0	95·2	Current grants to personal sector
16	6·3	0·0	6·3	0·0	6·3	Current grants abroad
17	57·6	−57·6	0·0	0·0	0·0	Current grants within public sector
18	24·5	0·7[3]	25·2	0·0	25·1	Debt interest
19			2·7	0·0	2·7	Apportionment of Reserve
20			**292·5**	**3·7**	**296·2**	**Total current expenditure**
21			**13·7**	**−0·2**	**13·5**	**Current deficit**
22	**0·0**	**0·3**	**0·3**	**0·0**	**0·2**	**Capital transfers**
						Capital expenditure[2]
23	4·7	5·7	10·4	5·7	16·2	Gross domestic fixed capital formation
24	−1·6	−4·9	−6·5	−3·8	−10·3	*Less* Depreciation
25	−0·1	0·0	−0·1	0·0	−0·1	Increase in stocks
26	4·2	1·2	5·4	0·4	5·8	Capital grants to private sector
27	6·6	−3·3	3·2	−3·2	0·0	Capital grants to public sector
28			0·3	0·0	0·3	Apportionment of Reserve
29			**12·7**	**−0·8**	**11·9**	**Total capital expenditure**
30			**26·1**	**−1·0**	**25·2**	**Financial deficit**
						Financial transactions
31	1·2	−0·3	0·9	0·0	0·9	Net lending to private sector and abroad
32	−3·0	0·0	−3·0	0·0	−3·0	Cash expenditure on company securities (including privatisation proceeds)
33	0·7	0·0	0·7	0·0	0·7	Transactions concerning certain public sector pension schemes
34	3·0	−0·1	2·9	0·0	2·9	Accruals adjustments on receipts
35	−1·5	−0·1	−1·6	−1·2	−2·8	Other accruals adjustments
36	−1·0	−0·8	−1·9	−0·5	−2·4	Miscellaneous financial transactions
37			**24·2**[4]	**−2·7**	**21·5**	**Borrowing requirement**

Changes to forecasts 4A.9 Table 4A.7 provides detail of changes to the public finance forecasts for 1994–95 and 1995–96 since the last Budget and since the Summer Economic Forecast. Previous forecasts have been adjusted for subsequent classification changes (see Annex A to Chapter 6, paragraph 6A.7). Full tax-by-tax details of the effects of the Budget measures are set out in Table 5.1, and a breakdown of the Control Total changes by department is shown in Table 6.5.

Table 4A.7 Comparison with previous forecasts[1]

	£ billion			
	Changes since last Budget		Changes since Summer Economic Forecast	
	1994–95	1995–96	1994–95	1995–96
Expenditure				
Control Total	−1·3	−6·9	−1·3	−6·9
Other general government expenditure[2]	−0·8	−1·2	−0·7	−0·5
Public corporations' market and overseas borrowing	−0·1	+0·4	−0·4	+0·1
Privatisation proceeds[3]	−0·8	−2·0	−0·8	−0·5
Total expenditure	**−3·0**	**−9·6**	**−3·1**	**−7·8**
Receipts				
Inland Revenue	+1·5	+0·6	+0·6	+0·6
Customs and Excise	−0·7	−0·8	−0·6	−0·6
Social security contributions	−0·3	−0·9	−0·4	−1·1
Other receipts	−0·4	−0·1	−1·4	−0·7
Total receipts	**0·0**	**−1·3**	**−1·8**	**−1·9**
PSBR	**−3·0**	**−8·4**	**−1·2**	**−6·0**

[1] Previous forecasts have been adjusted for classification changes.
[2] Excluding privatisation proceeds.
[3] A minus sign indicates higher privatisation proceeds.

Historical series for the PSBR and its main components

4A.10 Table 4A.8 sets out historical series for the PSBR and its main components, including GGE excluding privatisation proceeds, as shown in Chart 4.4. Table 4A.9 shows further details for government receipts, including the historical series for total taxes and social security contributions, shown in Chart 4.3.

Table 4A.8 Historical series for the PSBR and its components

	Per cent of money GDP					
	GGE excluding privatisation proceeds	Privatisation proceeds	GGE	General government receipts	Public corporations' market and overseas borrowing	**PSBR**
1965–66	37¾	0	37¾	35¼	0	2¾
1966–67	39½	0	39½	36¼	0	3
1967–68	43¼	0	43¼	38	–¼	5
1968–69	41½	0	41½	40¾	0	¾
1969–70	41	0	41	41¾	–½	–1¼
1970–71	41¼	0	41¼	40¼	½	1½
1971–72	41¾	0	41¾	39¾	–¼	1¾
1972–73	41½	0	41½	38	0	3¾
1973–74	43½	0	43½	38½	1	6
1974–75	48¾	0	48¾	40½	¾	9
1975–76	49¼	0	49¼	40¼	¼	9½
1976–77	46¾	0	46¾	41	¾	6½
1977–78	43¼	¼	43	39¾	¼	3½
1978–79	44	0	44	38¾	¼	5½
1979–80	44	¼	44	38¾	–¼	4¾
1980–81	46½	0	46½	40¾	–½	5¼
1981–82	47¼	¼	47	43¾	0	3¼
1982–83	47½	¼	47¼	43¾	–½	3¼
1983–84	46½	¼	46¼	42¾	0	3¼
1984–85	46¾	¾	46¼	43½	¼	3
1985–86	45	¾	44¼	42¼	–¼	1½
1986–87	44	1¼	42¾	41½	–¼	1
1987–88	41¾	1¼	40½	41	–¼	–¾
1988–89	39¼	1½	37¾	40¼	–½	–3
1989–90	39¾	¾	38¾	40	–¼	–1½
1990–91	40¼	1	39¼	39¼	0	0
1991–92	42	1¼	40¾	38¼	0	2½
1992–93	44½	1¼	43	36¾	–¼	6
1993–94	44¼	¾	43½	36	–¼	7
1994–95	43½	1	42½	37¼	–¼	5
1995–96	42½	½	42	38¾	–¼	3
1996–97	41¾	½	41¼	39¼	–¼	1¾
1997–98	41	¼	40¾	39¾	–¼	¾
1998–99	40	0	39¾	39¾	0	0
1999–2000	39¼	0	39¼	40	0	–1

Table 4A.9 Historical series for government receipts

	Per cent of money GDP				
	Total taxes and NICs	Other receipts	**General government receipts**	Non-North Sea taxes and NICs[1]	Public sector current receipts
1965–66	31¾	3½	**35¼**	31¾	37½
1966–67	32½	3¾	**36¼**	32½	38¼
1967–68	34	4	**38**	34	39¾
1968–69	35¾	5	**40¾**	35¾	42
1969–70	37½	4¼	**41¾**	37½	43¾
1970–71	37	3¼	**40¼**	37	42¾
1971–72	35¼	4½	**39¾**	35¼	41
1972–73	33	5	**38**	33	38¾
1973–74	33¾	4¾	**38½**	33¾	40
1974–75	36¼	4¼	**40½**	36¼	43
1975–76	36¾	3½	**40¼**	36¾	43¼
1976–77	36¼	4¾	**41**	36½	43¾
1977–78	35¼	4½	**39¾**	35½	42
1978–79	34¼	4½	**38¾**	34¾	41
1979–80	35½	3¼	**38¾**	35½	41¾
1980–81	36¾	4	**40¾**	36½	43
1981–82	39¾	3¾	**43¾**	39¼	46½
1982–83	39½	4¼	**43¾**	38½	46
1983–84	39	3¾	**42¾**	38¼	45
1984–85	39¾	3¾	**43½**	38¼	44½
1985–86	38¾	3½	**42¼**	37¼	44
1986–87	38¼	3¼	**41½**	37¾	42¾
1987–88	38¼	2¾	**41**	38	42½
1988–89	37½	2¾	**40¼**	37¼	41½
1989–90	37	3	**40**	37	40¾
1990–91	37	2¼	**39¼**	37	39¾
1991–92	36½	2	**38¼**	36¾	39
1992–93	34½	2¼	**36¾**	34¾	37¼
1993–94	33¾	2¼	**36**	34	36¼
1994–95	35¼	2	**37¼**	35¾	37¾
1995–96	36¾	2	**38¾**	37	39¼
1996–97	37¼	2	**39¼**	37½	39¾
1997–98	37¾	2	**39¾**	38	40
1998–99	38	2	**39¾**	38¼	40¼
1999–2000	38	2	**40**	38¼	40¼

[1] As a percent of non-North Sea GDP.

Annex B to Chapter 4
Conventions used in presenting the public finances

4B.1 The FSBR presents the public finances in two main ways; on a cash basis and on a national accounts, or accruals, basis. This Annex briefly describes the two approaches and outlines the relationships between the various public finances tables in Chapters 1, 4, 5 and 6.

4B.2 An important point to note at the outset is that the key expenditure and receipts aggregates, general government expenditure (GGE) and general government receipts (GGR), are national accounts concepts. But they can be disaggregated on both a national accounts basis and on a largely cash basis.

Cash basis

4B.3 The cash approach concentrates on the actual cash transactions between the public sector and the rest of the economy in any given period of time. It is particularly useful for analysing the components of the PSBR, which is itself almost entirely a cash concept. A cash basis also corresponds closely to the way public expenditure is planned, controlled and accounted for at present.

Tables 1.6, 4.1, 4.4 and 6.4   **4B.4** The main – albeit summary – presentation of the public finances on a cash basis is given in Tables 1.6 and 4.1. Supporting disaggregation of the Control Total is shown in Table 6.4, while Tables 4.4 and 4A.1 provide breakdowns of general government receipts.

4B.5 As far as possible, the figures in these tables relate to actual cash flows. The estimates of taxes for example are for tax payments received during the year, rather than for liabilities incurred. There are however, a number of items which are not on a cash basis:

- "social security contributions" are scored gross of amounts netted off by employers as reimbursement in respect of statutory sick pay and statutory maternity pay. These payments count as expenditure rather than negative receipts;

- VAT refunded to central and local government is included in "other taxes and royalties" (Table 4.4 and Table 4A.1);

- an imputed flow for capital consumption by general government is included in "other receipts" (Table 4.4 and Table 4A.1).

These latter two flows have no impact on the PSBR as they also appear on the expenditure side of the account in "accounting adjustments" (Table 1.6). This line also includes various other adjustments needed to get back to the national accounts basis required for GGE.

4B.6 The final departure from a cash basis is the "central government debt interest" line of Table 1.6, which scores the capital uplift on index-linked gilts as interest at the time it accrues. Because the PSBR is on a cash basis, an offset is made in the form of an accruals adjustment to "other receipts" (Table 4A.1). This removes the accrued uplift scored and adds back any actual payments of uplift on redemptions.

4B.7 Tables 1.5 and 4.5 are on the same basis as Table 1.6.

Table 4A.3 **4B.8** The other cash-based table is Table 4A.3, which shows the finances of central government. Unlike the earlier tables, this is genuinely a cash presentation, based on information from central government funds and accounts. The imputed flows for refunded VAT, social security contributions and capital consumption are all excluded, and the "interest payments" line takes account of actual payments of capital uplift on index-linked gilts, rather than the accrued uplift.

4B.9 Similar tables cannot be produced for local authorities or public corporations because the available cash data are not comprehensive. The finances of these sectors, shown in Tables 4A.4 and 4A.5, are presented on the national accounts basis described below.

National accounts basis

4B.10 The national accounts are produced by the CSO for the UK as a whole using an internationally agreed framework. Public finances shown on this basis can thus be placed more easily into the context of the rest of the economy, highlighting the inter-relationships between different sectors.

Table 4A.6 **4B.11** Table 4A.6 gives a detailed national accounts presentation of the short-term forecasts for the public finances. Under the measurement conventions used in the national accounts:

- most transactions, including most taxes (although not corporation tax), are recorded on an accruals rather than a cash payments basis;

- transactions are grouped by economic category. So, for example, transfer payments are distinguished from expenditure on goods and services;

- the value of some transactions is imputed where no money changes hands (for example, non-trading capital consumption).

4B.12 The public sector financial deficit is the balance between expenditure and income in the combined current and capital accounts (line 30 of Table 4A.6). Unlike the PSBR, the financial deficit is not wholly a measure of cash transactions because certain items above line 30 are measured on an accruals basis. The appropriate accruals adjustments are made in lines 34 and 35. Certain other financial transactions, notably net lending and privatisation proceeds, are also excluded from the financial deficit, but included in the PSBR.

4B.13 As the national accounts distinguish between current and capital transactions, they provide the natural framework in which to identify the current balance and capital spending. The current and capital breakdown shown in Table 4A.6 differs from the usual national accounts conventions in two respects. First, capital taxes (line 3) are counted as current rather than capital receipts on the grounds that they are not strictly speaking pure taxes on capital. And second, an estimate of depreciation is deducted from capital expenditure and added to current expenditure.

4B.14 GGE can be derived from the general government column of Table 4A.6 by taking current expenditure (line 20) plus capital expenditure (line 29) and adding:

- the Reserve (lines 19 and 28, all assumed to be general government);
- net lending to the private sector and abroad (line 31);
- cash expenditure on company securities (line 32);
- and net lending by central government to public corporations (£0·4 billion in 1994–95 and minus £1·0 billion in 1995–96).

4B.15 Correspondingly, GGR comprises general government current receipts (line 11) plus capital transfers (line 22), less:

- transactions concerning public sector pension schemes (line 33);
- accruals adjustments (lines 34 and 35);
- miscellaneous financial transactions (line 36).

Tables 1.1 and 4.2 **4B.16** A summary version of the public sector column of Table 4A.6 provides the framework for Tables 1.1 and 4.2. So, for example, "receipts" and "current expenditure" in these tables correspond to lines 11 and 20 of Table 4A.6. "Public sector net capital spending" represents the balance on the capital account: that is, total capital expenditure (line 29 of Table 4A.6) net of capital transfers (line 22). GGE and GGR cannot be derived from Table 1.1 because it show figures for the public sector, rather than just general government, and because it gives insufficient detail of the various financial transactions.

4B.17 Tables 1.1 and 4.2 show the current balance in the same way as Table 4A.6. Tables 4A.4 and 4A.5 are also on a national accounts basis.

Table 4A.9 **4B.18** An accruals basis is used to calculate taxes (and social security contributions and council tax) as a percent of GDP (Table 4A.9), because this gives a measure of the underlying burden of taxation stemming from a particular period of economic activity. It is not affected, for example, by the precise timing of tax receipts.

Tables 4A.4 and 4A.5   **4B.19**   Table 4A.6 shows local authorities' self-financed expenditure (net of their receipts from central government – line 17) and their receipts from outside the public sector (net of debt interest payments to central government – line 9). Table 4A.4, in contrast, provides figures for total local authority expenditure and receipts. It also gives a summary presentation of the income and expenditure flows in the local authority accounts, which it is not practical to put together from any other sources.

4B.20   Table 4A.5 serves the same purposes for public corporations as Table 4A.4 does for local authorities. Because public corporations are trading bodies, the national accounts presentation is a little different from that for general government. Most current expenditure is netted off from income to leave the gross trading surplus (shown under receipts). The expenditure side of the account only shows interest, dividend and tax payments, plus capital spending.

Borrowing requirements

4B.21   The PSBR can be disaggregated into component borrowing requirements in different ways. Tables 1.6 and 4.1 shows the PSBR as the sum of the general government borrowing requirement (GGBR) and market and overseas borrowing by public corporations (PCMOB). An alternative is to split it, as in Table 4A.2 and Table 4A.6 (line 37), between central government borrowing on its own account (the CGBR(O)), and borrowing by local authorities and public corporations (the LABR and PCBR respectively). The borrowing requirement shown in the general government column of Table 4A.6 is not in fact the GGBR, but the GGBR(O). The GGBR can be calculated from the GGBR(O) by adding in public corporations' borrowing from central government (given in paragraph 4B.14).

Public sector debt

4B.22   Table 4.3 sets out projections for two different measures of public sector debt. Net public sector debt is the stock analogue of the PSBR. It measures the public sector's financial liabilities to the private sector and abroad, net of short-term financial assets.

4B.23   Gross general government debt is the measure of debt used in the European Union's excessive deficits procedure. As a general government measure, it excludes the debt of public corporations. It measures general government's total financial liabilities, before netting off short-term financial assets.

5 The Budget tax and national insurance measures

5.01 This chapter summarises the tax and national insurance proposals in the Budget. The measures raise the main tax allowances and thresholds in line with prices, with extra increases for the elderly and in the lower rate tax band. Fuel and tobacco duties are increased in real terms in line with previous commitments, while most alcohol duties are frozen. There are a number of proposals to encourage investment in small and growing businesses, to help businesses facing higher rates bills, to simplify and deregulate the tax system and to close loopholes.

5.02 Overall the measures will cost some £1 billion in 1995–96, due mainly to transitional support on business rates. By 1997-98 the cost falls to under £½ billion, so the measures do not have a significant effect on revenues in the medium term.

5.03 The effect of the measures on government revenues is set out in Table 5.1[1]. Annex A explains the costings and Annex B details a number of tax changes which were announced before the Budget, including measures announced in the two 1993 Budgets but not yet implemented.

Inland Revenue taxes

Personal taxation **5.04** The following allowances, limits and thresholds will be increased in line with statutory indexation (based on the 2·2 per cent increase in the Retail Prices Index in the year to September 1994):

- personal allowance for people under 65 (1);
- income limit for age related allowances (3);
- basic rate limit (5);
- capital gains tax annual exempt amount (–);
- threshold for inheritance tax (6).

---

[1] *The number in brackets after each proposal refers to the line in Table 5.1 where its yield or cost is shown. The symbol "–" means the proposal has no effect on revenue; "★" means it has a negligible effect amounting to less than £3 million a year.*

5 The Budget tax and national insurance measures

5.05 Personal allowances for people aged 65 and over will be increased by £430, which is £330 more than indexation (2). The lower rate band will be increased by £200, £100 more than indexation (4). The blind person's allowance is unchanged (−). The new levels are as follows:

Income tax allowances (£)	1994–95	1995–96
Personal allowance	3 445	3 525
Married couple's allowance, additional personal allowance, widow's bereavement allowance	1 720	1 720[1]
For people aged 65–74:		
personal allowance	4 200	4 630
married couple's allowance	2 665	2 995[1]
For people aged 75 and over:		
personal allowance	4 370	4 800
married couple's allowance	2 705	3 035[1]
Income limit for age related allowances	14 200	14 600
Blind person's allowance	1 200	1 200

[1] *Announced in November 1993 Budget. See Annex B.*

Bands of taxable income (£)	1994–95	1995–96
Lower rate − 20 per cent	0 − 3 000	0 − 3 200
Basic rate − 25 per cent	3 001 − 23 700	3 201 − 24 300
Higher rate − 40 per cent	over 23 700	over 24 300

Other allowances and thresholds (£)	1994–95	1995–96
CGT annual exempt amount:		
individuals	5 800	6 000
trusts	2 900	3 000
Inheritance tax threshold	150 000	154 000

5.06 Changes will be made in the tax treatment of premiums paid for employee indemnity insurance such as directors' and officers' liability insurance. Where employers pay, the payment will not be taxable as a benefit in kind; where employees pay, they will get tax relief. The same treatment will apply to payments made to meet work related liabilities, such as legal costs, which are not covered by insurance; and to payments made up to six years after the end of the year in which the employment ends. This will take effect from 6 April 1995 (7).

5.07 The rules for registered profit related pay schemes will be amended to reflect changes in accountancy practice on extraordinary items (−).

5 The Budget tax and national insurance measures

Benefits in kind **5.08** The scales for assessing the benefit of fuel provided by employers for private use in company cars will be increased from 6 April 1995 by 5 per cent for petrol cars and 4 per cent for diesel cars, in line with the price of fuel (8). The scales are also used for employers' national insurance contributions (54) and VAT (27).

5.09 Accessories for the disabled, fitted in company cars, will not be taxed as a benefit in kind from 6 April 1995 (★).

Self assessment **5.10** Measures to simplify the personal tax system and allow self assessment were announced in the March 1993 Budget. Further measures which build on this framework are:

- all income from property, including furnished lettings, will be brought together and taxed using rules similar to those for trading income;

- the rules for taxing non-residents will be simplified;

- employers will be required to give employees certain information, mainly about benefits and expenses, which they need to complete their tax returns; and

- anti-avoidance provisions will be introduced to prevent exploitation of the rules for the transition from the 'preceding year' to the 'current year' basis of assessment (★).

Simplification and deregulation **5.11** Employees' personal expenses of up to £5 a night in the UK and £10 a night abroad, paid by employers when employees stay away from home on business, will not be taxable from 6 April 1995 (9).

5.12 Other simplification and deregulation changes are:

- the rules for taxation of trusts and other settlements which tax the settlor on the income of a settlement in certain circumstances will be simplified from 6 April 1995 (★);

- tax will be deducted at the basic rate from interest credited to bank accounts belonging to discretionary and accumulation trusts from 6 April 1996 (★);

- two changes will be made to simplify the offshore funds legislation from 29 November 1994 (★);

- measures will be introduced to allow certain tax returns to be submitted electronically (–);

- in Scotland, Inland Revenue will be able to pursue debts of up to £50,000 through the Sheriff courts rather than the Court of Session (–);

- the tax rules relating to foreign income dividends and certain forms of deemed income received by personal representatives of deceased persons' estates, and to payments made out of that income to residuary beneficiaries, will be clarified from 6 April 1995 (★).

5 The Budget tax and national insurance measures

Savings **5.13** Changes will be made to the rules for Tax Exempt Special Savings Accounts (TESSA) so that when an account matures after five years, up to £9,000 of the capital may be deposited in a new TESSA. The normal limit for first year deposits is £3,000 (10).

5.14 Personal Equity Plans (PEPs) will be extended to corporate bonds and preference shares (11).

5.15 The annual amount which may be invested in a friendly society tax exempt life assurance fund will be increased from £200 to £270 with effect from Royal Assent (★).

5.16 The maximum level of earnings for which pension provision may be made with tax relief (the "earnings cap") will be increased in line with statutory indexation to £78,600 (★).

5.17 Other savings measures are:

- investors in personal pension schemes will be given more flexibility to choose when to buy an annuity (★); and to buy annuities from insurance companies established in other European Union countries (–);

- the ordinary Save As You Earn (SAYE) scheme will be abolished. Contracts starting on or after 1 December 1994 will not get tax relief (★). The Sharesave scheme will continue, and the Treasury will take on responsibility for the model scheme from the Department for National Savings (–);

- financial institutions in other European Union countries will be able to offer PEPs, TESSAs and Sharesave SAYE schemes in the UK (★);

- gains made by higher rate taxpayers on certain life assurance policies and life annuity contracts written by insurers established in other European countries will in future only be charged on the difference between the higher and basic rates of tax (★).

Investment in small businesses **5.18** As announced in the November 1993 Budget, tax reliefs will be available to investors in Venture Capital Trusts (VCTs), a new vehicle designed to encourage investment in unquoted trading companies. Investors will benefit from income tax relief at 20 per cent, and capital gains tax reinvestment relief, on purchase of new VCT shares of up to £100,000 a year. Income and gains on these investments will also be tax free (12).

5.19 Relief from capital gains tax which is available where gains are reinvested in an unquoted trading company will, from 29 November 1994, be extended to cover companies which are engaged in farming or developing property, or which hold more than half their assets in land and buildings (13).

5.20 The reliefs available under the Enterprise Investment Scheme will be extended to allow CGT to be deferred on capital gains where they are reinvested in a company which qualifies under the scheme. Changes will also be made to simplify the scheme and make it more attractive for companies and investors to use. These include allowing relief when more than half a company's assets are in land and buildings (14).

Business taxation

5.21 Tax relief will be given for certain spending by individuals after their trade or profession has ceased. The relief will apply to spending on or after 29 November 1994 (15).

5.22 Employers will be allowed to make quarterly rather than monthly payments of PAYE and national insurance contributions from 6 April 1995 when their total PAYE and NIC bill is below £600 a month, an increase from the current threshold of £450 (16, 55).

5.23 The industrial buildings allowance provisions will be amended to extend capital allowances to design, build, finance and operate (DBFO) roads; and new rules will give capital allowances balancing charges to them and to toll roads covered by the private finance initiative (17).

5.24 Other business taxation changes are:

- the relief which allows group companies to set gains from the sale of business assets against the cost of assets acquired by other companies in the same group will be put on a statutory basis (–);

- the stamp duty relief for sales of property within a group of companies will be extended to new leases, and the test for group membership for the purposes of this relief will be revised from 90 per cent ownership of issued share capital to 75 per cent ownership of ordinary share capital, from Royal Assent (★);

- changes will be made to facilitate the use of cash as collateral for stock loans and to address anomalies in the interaction between the legislation on sale and repurchase of securities in the Finance Act 1994 and other legislation (★);

- a tax regime will be established for open ended investment companies, a new form of collective investment vehicle which will be constituted as a company with continuously variable share capital. It is expected that the necessary secondary legislation will be brought into effect by mid-1995 (★);

- the distribution rules applying to thinly capitalised companies will be modified (★);

- the tax treatment of short rotation coppice (in which fast growing trees are regularly harvested for fuel) will be clarified to ensure that it is taxed as farming and thus excluded from the exemption for commercial woodlands (★).

5 The Budget tax and national insurance measures

Anti-avoidance and revenue protection measures

5.25 Returns on certain debt instruments such as deep discount bonds held by UK companies associated with companies carrying on a banking business in the UK will be taxed as they accrue, rather than on sale or maturity, from 29 November 1994. There will be no change where the instruments are held for long-term insurance purposes (18).

5.26 From 29 November 1994 companies within a group will only be able to claim rollover relief for business assets acquired from outside that group and not by transfer from other companies within the same group (19). Changes from the same date will also counter avoidance of the charge which applies when a company leaves a group holding an asset which it acquired from another company in the same group (★).

5.27 Changes will be made to prevent avoidance of tax by manipulating the valuation of stock when a trade is transferred between connected parties (20).

5.28 Where there is a change in the ownership of an investment company, measures will be introduced to prevent companies setting excess management expenses and charges from the period before the change against profits of a later period. This will apply to changes in ownership on or after 29 November 1994, unless the contract for sale was entered into before that date (21).

5.29 Any petroleum revenue tax (PRT) losses transferred to the purchaser of an interest in an oil or gas field will exclude losses attributable to reliefs brought into the field by the seller. Reliefs brought into a field will also be excluded from any unrelievable field loss which is set against the PRT liability of another field. The changes apply to claims for relief and transfers of an interest made on or after 29 November 1994 (22).

5.30 Measures will be introduced to prevent erosion of the tax base for life assurance companies through reinsurance arrangements, and to correct other anomalies (23).

5.31 Measures will also be introduced to:

- ensure that capital gains tax applies to disposals of certain securities linked to a share index, on or after 29 November 1994 (★);

- amend the capital allowances rules for industrial buildings and buildings in enterprise zones to clarify the amounts on which allowances can be claimed (–);

- amend the provisions introduced in the March 1993 Budget for Lloyd's special reserve funds to ensure that they operate as originally intended (–).

Customs and Excise taxes

Value added tax **5.32** The annual turnover threshold above which traders must register for VAT will increase from £45,000 to £46,000 and the deregistration threshold will rise from £43,000 to £44,000, from midnight on 29 November 1994 (★).

5.33 From 1 August 1995 businesses will be able to recover VAT on the purchase of cars bought wholly for business use, primarily leasing. Where VAT is recoverable, businesses will have to account for output tax on the eventual sale of the car by the business. Only half of the VAT applying to leasing charges will be recoverable where there is any private use (24).

5.34 The scheme under which VAT on certain second-hand goods is charged only on the dealer's margin will be extended to virtually all second-hand goods, antiques and collectors' items, whether sold by a dealer or at public auction. A simplified method of global accounting for some margin scheme transactions will be introduced, and an effective VAT rate of 2·5 per cent will be charged on imports of certain works of art, antiques and collectors' items which were previously exempted from VAT at import. These changes implement the European Community seventh VAT directive and will be phased in from 1 January 1995 (25).

5.35 The zero-rating of passenger transport will be confined to public passenger transport in the generally accepted sense, as envisaged when the relief was first introduced, from 1 April 1995 (26).

5 The Budget tax and national insurance measures

5.36 A number of changes will be made to reduce burdens on business:

- traders will be consulted on a move to annual VAT returns and payments for small businesses. Subject to views expressed, it is envisaged that those who voluntarily register for VAT will make annual returns by the end of 1995, with a possible extension to businesses with an annual turnover below £100,000 the following year. There will also be consultation on a simplified scheme for calculating VAT due from small businesses, which would link payments to turnover rather than to detailed accounts of all sales and purchases (–);

- a number of deregulatory measures associated with the VAT liability of construction and land and property will be introduced. Most will take effect from 1 March 1995 (28);

- the penalties for late VAT registration, unauthorised issue of tax invoices, and failure to notify import of new means of transport or goods liable to excise duty and pay the VAT on time, will be reduced to bring them into line with other VAT penalties, from 1 January 1995 (29);

- the VAT bad debt relief provisions of the VAT Act 1994 will be clarified, and from Royal Assent Customs' right to deduct traders' debts from VAT credits arising during insolvency will be limited further (★);

- the long-standing practice of allowing payment of VAT due on goods removed from excise warehouses to be deferred will be put on a statutory basis from Royal Assent (–).

5.37 A number of changes will be made to reduce scope for avoidance of VAT:

- the rules will be changed to stop avoidance of VAT through lease and lease back of property from 30 November 1994 (30);

- the rules on incidental financial transactions will be changed to block a device used to avoid VAT on share issues from 1 December 1994 (31);

- to counter abuse, the de minimis rules which determine when small businesses making exempt supplies can treat themselves as fully taxable will be tightened from 1 December 1994 (32);

- traders appealing against a Customs requirement to provide security against payment of their VAT liability will have to be up to date with their VAT returns and payments, from Royal Assent (33);

- section 30(5) of the VAT Act 1994 will be repealed from Royal Assent to prevent it being used as a basis for tax avoidance. Alternative legislative cover will be provided to allow registered charities to continue to reclaim VAT on goods exported for charitable purposes (–).

Excise duties 5.38 Duty on beer, table wine, cider and spirits will remain unchanged (34, 35, 38). Duty on fortified wine will be reduced from 1 January 1995 in line with a previous international agreement (37). The duty on sparkling wine will be reduced to the new fortified wine rate at the same time (36).

5.39 Duties on tobacco products will be increased from 6 pm on 29 November 1994, in line with the Government's commitment to increase duty on average by at least 3 per cent a year in real terms (39).

5.40 Tax on petrol will rise by 2·5 pence per litre, and duty on diesel will rise to bring it into line with that for unleaded petrol, from 6 pm on 29 November 1994, in line with the Government's commitment to increase duty on road fuels on average by at least 5 per cent a year in real terms (40, 41, 42). Duty on gas oil and fuel oil will rise by 0·5 pence per litre from the same time (43).

5.41 The changes in duty and their effect on the price of each product are set out below. Price effects include VAT except for gas oil and fuel oil.

Excise duty changes				
	Change in duty (per cent)	Effect on price of typical item (pence)	Unit	
Alcohol				
Beer	0	0	pint	(34)
Table wine	0	0	75cl bottle	(35)
Sparkling wine	−13·5	−27	75cl bottle	(36)
Fortified wine	−7·1	−13	75cl bottle	(37)
Cider and perry	0	0	2 litre	(★)
Spirits	0	0	70 cl bottle	(38)
Tobacco				
Cigarettes	5·5[1]	10	packet of 20	(39)
Cigars	6·4	5	packet of 5	(★)
Hand-rolling tobacco	5·0	12	25 grams	(★)
Pipe tobacco	6·0	6	25 grams	(★)
Fuel				
Leaded petrol	6·4	2·5	litre	(40)
Unleaded petrol	7·5	2·5	litre	(41)
Diesel	9·9	3·2	litre	(42)
Gas oil	30·5	0·5	litre	(43)
Fuel oil	43·1	0·5	litre	(43)

[1] *Specific duty up 6.2 per cent. Rate of ad valorem duty unchanged.*

5.42 The rate of duty on road fuel gas will remain at its current level, but will be expressed per kilogram rather than per litre from 6 pm on 29 November 1994 (★).

5.43 The rules for giving duty relief to traders using mineral oil for industrial purposes other than as motor or heating fuel will be changed to reduce the administrative burden on traders from the summer of 1995 (★).

5.44 The definition of vehicles entitled to use rebated heavy oil (commonly known as red diesel) as fuel on public roads will be revised to preserve nearly all existing entitlements following changes to vehicle excise duty, from 1 July 1995 (★).

5.45 A number of changes will be made to simplify the structure of alcohol duties:

- the number of tax bands for wine and made-wine with strength between 1·2 and 5·5 per cent alcohol by volume (abv) will be reduced from five to two from 1 January 1995 (★);

- the systems for refunding duty on alcohol used in the manufacture of food and non-alcoholic drinks will be unified and simplified from Royal Assent (★);

- the regime for denatured alcohol, including methylated spirits, will be extended to cover all dutiable alcohols used in foods and non-alcoholic drinks from the summer of 1995 (★);

- the definition of beverages between 1·2 and 5·5 per cent abv which are liable to beer duty rate will be clarified from 30 November 1994 (★).

5.46 A statutory right to recover excise duty which has been overpaid will be introduced; and there will be provision for claims to be brought before the VAT and Duties Tribunal in the event of an appeal, from the summer of 1995 (★).

5.47 Gaming machine licence duty will be increased on average by about 19 per cent for licence applications made on or after 1 December 1994, and payment by instalments will be introduced from 1 November 1995 for annual licences (44). From the latter date, the duty will be extended to include amusement machines and will be renamed amusement machine licence duty. (45).

5.48 A number of changes will be made to air passenger duty:

- treatment of debts in insolvency will be aligned with other duties and taxes collected by Customs, from Royal Assent (−); and

- a mechanism will be provided for the assessment and collection of interest on arrears from 1 January 1995 (★).

5 The Budget tax and national insurance measures

Insurance premium tax   **5.49** From Royal Assent, Customs' powers under the legislation for insurance premium tax will be aligned more closely with those available for other indirect taxes (−). In addition, the right of insurers to request a review and appeal against an assessment for tax due will be removed for cases where no tax return has been submitted (−).

Intrastat   **5.50** The threshold above which traders are required to submit monthly statistical returns on trade with European Union countries will be increased from £140,000 of annual EU trade in goods to £150,000, from 1 January 1995 (−).

Vehicle excise duty

5.51 Duty on cars, light goods vehicles, taxis and vans will rise from £130 to £135 from 30 November 1994 (46). Duty on lorries is unchanged (47).

5.52 The system of concessionary and exempt classes of VED will be rationalised with effect from 1 July 1995. The number of concessionary classes will be reduced from 132 to nine. Exemption from VED will be extended to police vehicles (48).

5.53 The definition of a goods vehicle for tax purposes and the taxable weight of such vehicles will be clarified (49).

5.54 A number of other changes will be made:

- new powers will be introduced to enable a fee, to cover the costs of the Driver and Vehicle Licensing Agency (DVLA), to be charged on new vehicle registrations which are not notified to DVLA under the automated first registration scheme (50);

- DVLA will be allowed to sell anonymised data, for example to market research companies (50);

- powers will be introduced to enable wheelclamping to be used to combat VED evasion (50);

- new requirements to provide documentation will be placed on the vendor, to reinforce the proposed move to joint notification of changes in vehicle ownership (−);

- vehicles with fewer than nine seats currently licensed as 'Hackney' carriages, will be licensed as cars from 1 July 1995 (★).

5 The Budget tax and national insurance measures

Business rates

Transitional relief 5.55 A revaluation of non-domestic properties will take effect across Great Britain from 1 April 1995. This will be the first five yearly review of property valuations for rating purposes following the introduction of the new business rating system.

5.56 Changes in rateable values resulting from revaluation will vary significantly between regions. A scheme of transitional relief will limit the maximum real increases in rates bills over the coming years to 10 per cent a year for large properties, 7½ per cent for small properties, and 5 per cent for small mixed domestic/non-domestic properties (such as shops with flats above).

5.57 The transitional relief scheme will be financed in 1995-96 in part by limiting real reductions in rates bills to 5 per cent for large properties and 10 per cent for small ones. An Exchequer contribution will cover the balance (51).

Rate poundages 5.58 The unified poundages in England and Wales for 1995–96 will be increased in line with the RPI for the year to September 1994, after account is taken of the effects of the revaluation. In Scotland a unified poundage will be introduced for the first time in 1995–96. It will be set at the same level as the poundage in England.

National insurance contributions

5.59 The lower rates of employers' national insurance contributions will be reduced by 0·6 per cent from April 1995 (52).

5.60 From April 1996 employers who take on someone who has been out of work for at least two years will be able to get a rebate on their employer NICs on that person for up to a year (53).

5 The Budget tax and national insurance measures

5.61 From April 1995 the lower earnings limit will be increased from £57 to £59 a week, in line with the single person's rate of retirement pension; the earnings thresholds for the employers' lower rate bands will each be increased by £5 to £105, £150 and £205; and the upper earnings limit will be increased from £430 to £440 a week (–). The new structure of contributions is:

Structure of national insurance contributions from April 1995

Weekly earnings	Percentage NIC rate[1] Employees	Employers[2]
Below £59	0	0·0
£59 to £104·99	2% of £59	3·0
£105 to £149·99	plus 10%	5·0
£150 to £204·99	of earnings	7·0
£205 to £440	between £59	10·2
Above £440	and £440	10·2

[1] *Not contracted out rates.*
[2] *Rates apply to all earnings.*

5.62 The weekly Class 2 rate for the self employed will be increased to £5·85, and the Class 3 voluntary contribution to £5·75. The lower and upper profits limits for Class 4 contributions will increase to £6,640 and £22,880 respectively (–).

5.63 To simplify the NICs system and provide a better service for business, Inland Revenue dispensations will count for NICs; and the Inland Revenue and the DSS will be drawing up a programme for closer working (–).

5.64 Treasury grant not exceeding 12·5 per cent of contributory benefit expenditure will be made available to the National Insurance Fund in 1995–96.

5.65 The Government Actuary will report on the likely effect of the changes on the National Insurance Fund. The working assumptions provided to the Government Actuary for use in preparing his report are set out in Annex A to Chapter 3.

5 The Budget tax and national insurance measures

Table 5.1 Direct effects of Budget measures

	£ million yield (+)/cost (−) of measure			
	Changes from a non-indexed base	Changes from an indexed base		
	1995–96	1995–96	1996–97	1997–98
INLAND REVENUE				
Personal taxation				
1 Personal allowance – indexed	−390	0	0	0
2 Age related personal allowances – up by £430	−200	−150	−210	−210
3 Income limit for age related allowances – indexed	−5	0	0	0
4 Lower rate band – up by £200	−170	−80	−100	−110
5 Basic rate limit – indexed	−160	0	0	0
6 Inheritance tax threshold – indexed	−15	0	0	0
7 Tax relief for employee indemnity insurance	−40	−40	−40	−40
8 Car fuel scales – increased in line with fuel prices	10	10	10	10
9 Personal incidental expenses – exempted	−20	−20	−20	−20
Savings				
10 TESSAs – extended	★	★	−150	−160
11 Personal Equity Plans – extended	−10	−10	−25	−40
Investment in small businesses				
12 Venture Capital Trusts	−150	−150	−290	−240
13 CGT reinvestment relief – changed	★	★	−15	−20
14 Enterprise Investment Scheme – extended	−5	−5	−10	−10
Business taxation				
15 Post-cessation expenditure – tax relief	★	★	−10	−10
16 PAYE – quarterly payments extended	−50	−50	★	★
17 Capital allowances – extended to DBFO roads	★	★	★	−5
Anti-avoidance measures				
18 Debt instruments – use restricted	20	20	100	100
19 Company groups – rollover relief	5	5	50	50
20 Valuation of stock – restricted	0	0	20	20
21 Management expenses buying	★	★	30	30
22 PRT loss transfer – restricted	25	25	25	25
23 Life assurance companies – reinsurance etc	50	50	−50	★
Total Inland Revenue	**−1 105**	**−395**	**−685**	**−630**
CUSTOMS AND EXCISE				
Value added tax				
24 Cars for business use – changed treatment	−140	−140	−100	−50
25 Second-hand goods and imported works of art	−60	−60	−55	−55
26 VAT on passenger transport – clarified	35	35	45	45
27 Car fuel scales – increased in line with fuel prices	10	10	10	10
VAT simplification and deregulation				
28 Land and property – simplification and deregulation	−60	−60	−60	−60
29 Penalties for late notification	−5	−5	★	★

5 The Budget tax and national insurance measures

Table 5.1 Direct effects of Budget measures—*continued*

	£ million yield (+)/cost (−) of measure			
	Changes from a non-indexed base	Changes from an indexed base		
	1995–96	1995–96	1996–97	1997–98
VAT anti-avoidance measures				
30 Land and property – blocking loopholes	210	210	215	215
31 Recovery of VAT on share issues restricted	100	100	100	100
32 Prevention of abuse of de minimis limits	20	20	20	20
33 Doubtful payers and appeals	10	10	0	0
Excise duties on:				
34 beer unchanged	0	−60	−60	−65
35 table wine unchanged	0	−15	−15	−20
36 sparkling wine down 13·5%	−5	−10	−10	−10
37 fortified wine down 7·1%	−5	−5	−5	−5
38 spirits unchanged	0	−15	−15	−15
39 cigarettes up 5.5%	15	15	15	20
40 leaded petrol up 6.4%	−40	−40	−40	−40
41 unleaded petrol up 7.5%	15	15	20	25
42 diesel up 9.9%	115	115	130	145
43 gas and fuel oils up 0.5p per litre	75	70	70	70
44 gaming machine licences up 19%	−30	−30	15	30
45 gaming machine licences – scope extended	10	10	30	35
Total Customs and Excise	**270**	**170**	**310**	**395**
VEHICLE EXCISE DUTY				
46 Duty on cars up £5 to £135	125	55	55	55
47 Duty on lorries unchanged	0	−10	−10	−10
48 Changes to exemptions and concessions	20	20	30	30
49 Definition of goods vehicle	5	5	5	5
50 Other changes	5	5	30	25
Total vehicle excise duty	**155**	**75**	**110**	**105**
BUSINESS RATES				
51 New transitional scheme	−605	−605	−135	−10
Total business rates	**−605**	**−605**	**−135**	**−10**
NATIONAL INSURANCE CONTRIBUTIONS				
52 Reduction of lower rates of employer NICs	−235	−235	−260	−265
53 Employer NIC rebate for long-term unemployed	0	0	−45	−45
54 Car fuel scales – increased in line with fuel prices	0	0	5	5
55 NICs – quarterly payments extended	−25	−25	★	★
Total national insurance contributions	**−260**	**−260**	**−300**	**−305**
TOTAL	**−1 545**	**−1 015**	**−700**	**−445**

★ = *Negligible*.

Annex A to Chapter 5
Explaining the costings

This annex explains how the effects of Budget measures on tax yield set out in Table 5.1 are calculated.

The general approach

5A.1 The direct effect of a tax change is the difference between the tax yield from applying the post-Budget and pre-Budget tax regimes to the levels of income, spending etc expected after the Budget.

5A.2 Since total income and total spending at factor cost are assumed to be fixed at their post-Budget levels, the estimates do not include any effect the tax changes themselves may have on levels of income and spending.

5A.3 Other effects on behaviour are taken into account where they are likely to have a significant effect on the yield. For example changes to excise duties influence the pattern of consumer spending.

5A.4 The estimates take account of any consequential changes in receipts from related taxes. For example, the estimated yield from increasing the excise duty on tobacco includes the change in the yield of VAT on that duty, and the change in the yield of VAT and other excise duties resulting from the new pattern of spending.

5A.5 The direct effect of some tax changes is affected by the implementation of others. Where this happens, measures are costed in the order in which they appear in Table 5.1.

5A.6 In the first column of the table the pre-Budget regime is the regime of allowances, thresholds and rates of duty which applied before this Budget (including any measures previously announced but not yet implemented).

5A.7 The remaining three columns strip out the effects of inflation by assuming that allowances, thresholds and rates of duty are increased in line with prices in this and in future Budgets (again taking account of measures previously announced but not yet implemented). Measures announced in this Budget are assumed to be indexed in the same way in future Budgets.

5A.8 In calculating the indexed base we assume that each year excise duties rise in December (January for alcohol), and allowances and thresholds rise in April, in line with the assumed increase in the RPI over twelve months to the previous September. The assumptions are 3 per cent, 2½ per cent and 2 per cent for September 1995, 1996 and 1997 respectively.

Notes on individual Budget measures

Inland Revenue taxes

1,3,5,6   The increases in allowances, thresholds and limits are rounded according to statutory rules after being increased in line with the rise in the all items Retail Prices Index in the year to September 1994.

2   The cost of the increase in a full year, against an indexed base, is £200 million.

4   The cost of the increase in a full year, against an indexed base, is £100 million.

18–23   The yield represents the estimated direct effect of the measures with the existing level of activity. Without these measures there could be a more significant loss of revenue in the future.

Customs and Excise taxes

37   The reduction in duty on fortified wines reflects the Government's intention, announced in December 1992, to reduce the duty differential between fortified wine and table wine.

39   This row shows the additional yield from the duty increases specified compared with the yield from raising duty by 3 per cent in real terms as announced in the November 1993 Budget. Since the commitment was expressed in real terms there is no difference between the indexed and non-indexed base.

40, 41, 42   These rows show the additional yield from the duty increases specified compared with the yield from raising duty by 5 per cent in real terms as announced in the November 1993 Budget. Since the commitment was expressed in real terms there is no difference between the indexed and non-indexed base.

44   Includes the cost of payment by instalments.

Revenue effects in 1994-95

A number of the Budget measures have effects on revenue in 1994-95. These are summarised below:

		£ million yield (+)/cost (−) of measure
		Changes from an indexed base
25	Second-hand goods and imported works of art	−10
30	Land and property – blocking certain loopholes	15
31	Recovery of VAT on share issues restricted	10
34–38	Alcohol duty	−20
39	Tobacco duty	5
40–42	Road fuel duties	25
43	Other fuels	20
44	Gaming machine licence duty	5
46–50	VED	15
	Total	**65**

Annex B to Chapter 5
Tax changes announced before the Budget

This annex sets out a number of tax changes which were announced before the Budget, the effects of which are taken into account in the forecasts.

Table 5B.1 Direct effect of measures announced since the November 1993 Budget

	£ million yield (+)/cost (−)			
	Changes from a non-indexed base	Changes from an indexed base		
	1995-96	1995-96	1996-97	1997-98
Inland Revenue taxes				
B1 Indexation of capital losses – transitional relief	−10	−10	−5	★
B2 Ships – rollover relief	−10	−10	−20	−20
B3 Construction industry tax scheme	0	0	0	★
Customs and Excise taxes				
B4 Zero rate on converted dwellings	−20	−20	−20	−20
B5 Revised VAT education exemption	−15	−15	−15	−15
National insurance contributions				
B6 Anti-avoidance measures	50	50	50	50
Total	−5	−5	−10	−5

★ = *Negligible.*

Inland Revenue taxes

5B.1 Transitional relief, up to a maximum of £10,000, is available to individuals and trusts for indexed capital losses realised between 30 November 1993 and 5 April 1995. The measure was announced in April 1994.

5B.2 It was announced on 21 April 1994 that balancing charges arising on the disposal of certain ships may be rolled over for a period of up to three years from the date of disposal. The charges will be set against subsequent expenditure on the acquisition of such ships within the period.

5B.3 The construction industry tax scheme will be modified following the move to self assessment. Only where sub-contractors are running genuine business operations will the contractor be exempt from the requirement to deduct tax from payments. The rate of deduction will be reduced; and deduction arrangements will be computerised. The changes will not take effect before the start of 1998–99.

Customs and Excise taxes

5B.4 An extra statutory concession was granted with effect from 21 July 1994 which extended VAT zero-rating to new dwellings created by conversion of non-residential buildings, and enabled builders to reclaim as input tax the VAT charged on certain electrical items incorporated into new dwellings.

Annex B to Chapter 5: Tax changes announced before the Budget

5B.5 An extra statutory concession was granted with effect from 1 August 1994 to replace the previous VAT exemption for fee paying education, training and research with a new exemption to simplify the relief and clarify the tax borderlines.

National insurance contributions

5B.6 From August 1994 employers have been liable to pay national insurance contributions on payments to their employees in the form of alcoholic liquors not subject to UK tax, or diamonds and other gemstones.

Table 5B.2 Direct effect of measures announced in the November 1993 Budget or earlier which do not take effect until after the November 1994 Budget

	£ million yield (+)/cost (−)			
	Changes from a non-indexed base	Changes from an indexed base		
	1995-96	1995-96	1996-97	1997-98
Inland Revenue taxes				
B7 Married couple's allowance etc – restricted to 15%	740	810	1 040	1 090
B8 Mortgage interest relief – restricted to 15%	880	880	910	950
B9 Incapacity benefit – tax new recipients from April 1995	50	50	110	160
B10 Self assessment	★	★	50	−250
Customs and Excise taxes				
B11 VAT on domestic fuel and power	1 020	1 020	1 525	1 540
B12 Road fuel duties to be increased by 5% real	1 240	925	1 820	2 835
B13 Tobacco duties to be increased by 3% real	375	240	455	685
Total	**4 305**	**3 925**	**5 910**	**7 010**

★ = *Negligible*.

Inland Revenue taxes

5B.7 From 6 April 1995 tax relief for the married couple's allowance, and allowances linked to it, will be restricted to 15 per cent. The married couple's allowance for those aged under 65 and the allowances linked to it will be £1,720. The married couple's allowance for those aged 65-74 will be £2,995 and for those aged 75 and over £3,035. Tax relief on the first £1,720 of maintenance payments will also be restricted to 15 per cent.

5B.8 From 6 April 1995 tax relief for mortgage interest payments will be restricted to 15 per cent. This will also reduce public spending on mortgage interest relief for borrowers who are non-taxpayers by £60 million a year. Relief will remain at 25 per cent for those aged 65 and over who take out loans to buy life annuities.

5B.9 Sickness and invalidity benefit will be replaced by incapacity benefit from 13 April 1995. Incapacity benefit will be taxable for new recipients from that date. The element of the benefit which replaces sickness benefit will not be taxed.

Annex B to Chapter 5: Tax changes announced before the Budget

5B.10 As announced in the March 1993 Budget, the assessment and collection of personal tax will be reformed from 1996-97 with the introduction of self assessment. The main measures abolish the 'preceding year' basis of assessment for the self employed, and tax income as it arises from 1997-98, with a transitional year in 1996-97; align payment dates for assessed income tax from all sources and for capital gains tax; introduce separate assessment for partners; and introduce clear rules for filing tax returns, allowing taxpayers the option of calculating their own tax, and for the payment of tax, and clear sanctions for failing to comply with them. After 1997-98 the measures are expected to produce a yield.

The November 1993 FSBR stated that stamp duties on securities, and on transfers of property other than land and buildings, would continue beyond 1993-94. It remains the intention to abolish stamp duties on securities etc in the longer term, but it is assumed that they will continue for the time being, and probably for a time after the introduction of the new system of paperless share trading known as Crest. The revenue forecasts therefore assume continuation of these receipts.

Customs and Excise taxes

5B.11 VAT will be charged on domestic fuel and power at the standard rate of 17·5 per cent from 1 April 1995, having been introduced at 8 per cent on 1 April 1994.

5B.12 The Chancellor said in the November 1993 Budget that road fuel duties would be increased on average by at least 5 per cent in real terms in future Budgets.

5B.13 The Chancellor said in the November 1993 Budget that tobacco duties would be increased on average by at least 3 per cent in real terms in future Budgets.

6 Public spending

Introduction

6.01 The Government's objective is to reduce public spending as a share of national income over time. The plans for public expenditure set out in this Budget are consistent with that objective.

6.02 The public expenditure survey covers the period from 1995–96 to 1997–98. In each year, the new plans are well below those announced in the last Financial Statement and Budget Report (FSBR). This reflects savings across most programmes, partly because the price level in 1995-96 and thereafter is now expected to be about 2½ per cent lower than assumed last year.

The Control Total

6.03 The Government's plans for public spending are set in terms of the Control Total (previously the New Control Total). This covers over 80 per cent of total spending. It excludes accounting adjustments and the two areas most affected by the economic cycle (cyclical social security and debt interest): these are included in general government expenditure, which is discussed in paragraphs 6.10 to 6.12.

1994–95   **6.04** The Control Total for the current year, 1994–95, is currently forecast at £249·6 billion, an underspend of £1·3 billion compared with the plans in the last Budget (after taking account of classification changes). Social security and local authority spending are forecast to be higher than planned, but that is more than covered by the Reserve of £3½ billion set last year. Elsewhere, there are minor changes in departments' expected levels of spending and an allowance for shortfall which reflects the Treasury's view that overall departments will underspend this year.

New plans   **6.05** The Control Totals for the next three years are set out in Table 6.1. They contain Reserves of £3 billion in 1995–96, £6 billion in 1996–97 and £9 billion in 1997–98.

6 Public spending

Table 6.1 The Control Total

	£ billion			
	1994–95	1995–96	1996–97	1997–98
Plans in November 1993 Budget after classification changes	250·8	262·6	271·7	281·0
New plans set out in this report	249·6	255·7	263·5	272·1
Reductions	–1·3	–6·9	–8·3	–8·9

Comparison with last Budget – cash

6.06 As Table 6.1 shows, the new plans are substantially below the figures in the last FSBR. This is the third successive Budget to reduce the spending plans set the year before. Chart 6.1 shows the successive reductions in plans. In cash terms the plans for 1995–96 have been reduced over the last two years by £8·3 billion compared with those originally set in the 1992 Survey.

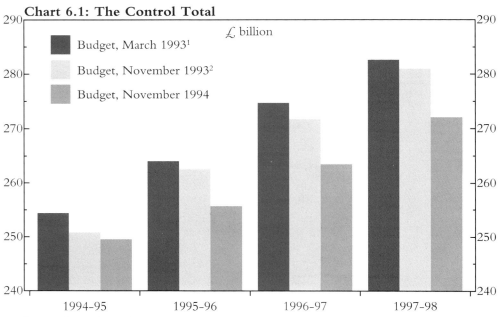

Chart 6.1: The Control Total

[1] Adjusted for classification changes. Projection for 1996-97 and 1997-98.
[2] Adjusted for classification changes. Projection for 1997-98.

Comparison with last Budget – real

6.07 Chart 6.2 shows the new plans in real terms – ie adjusted by the GDP deflator to exclude the effects of general inflation. Because inflation in the current year has been lower than expected at the time of the last Budget, the real level of spending in 1994–95 is higher than planned last year. But the plans for the next three years are lower in real terms than those published last year.

Real growth

6.08 Year on year, the Control Total in 1995–96 is expected to be about 0·8 per cent lower in real terms than in 1994–95. The plans then imply real terms increases of ½ per cent in 1996–97 and 1 per cent in 1997–98. These figures are also shown in Table 1.5. Average real growth over the three year Survey period is less than ¼ per cent a year, well below the ceiling of 1½ per cent established by the Government in 1992.

6 Public spending

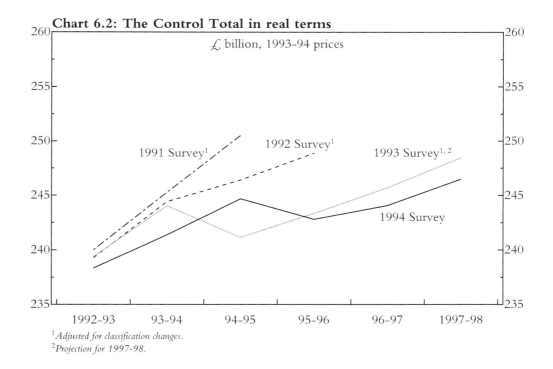

Chart 6.2: The Control Total in real terms

[1] Adjusted for classification changes.
[2] Projection for 1997-98.

Other expenditure measures

6.09 Some measures taken in this Budget directly affect public expenditure outside the Control Total. In particular there are measures which reduce cyclical social security, as described in paragraph 6.73. Taking account of these, the overall Budget changes in public expenditure are set out in Table 6.2.

Table 6.2 Total Budget changes in public expenditure

	£ billion		
	1995–96	1996–97	1997–98
Cash terms			
Control Total	−6·9	−8·3	−8·9
Cyclical social security measures[1]	−0·4	−0·7	−0·9
Total Budget changes	**−7·2**	**−9·0**	**−9·8**
Real terms[2]			
Control Total[3]	−0·5	−1·6	−2·0
Cyclical social security measures	−0·3	−0·6	−0·8
Total Budget changes	**−0·9**	**−2·3**	**−2·8**

[1] See paragraph 6.73.
[2] 1993–94 prices.
[3] Change in real terms Control Totals

6 Public spending

General Government expenditure

6.10 A detailed analysis of general government expenditure excluding privatisation proceeds (GGE) is set out in Table 6.3. In total, GGE is expected to be some £28 billion lower over the years 1995–96 to 1997–98 than projected in last year's FSBR. Chart 6.3 shows that the ratio of GGE to GDP is projected to be lower throughout the period than expected in the last Budget.

Table 6.3 The Control Total and general government expenditure (excluding privatisation proceeds)[1]

	£ million							
	Outturn	Estimated outturn	New plans/projections			Changes from previous plans/projections		
	1993–94	1994–95	1995–96	1996–97	1997–98	1994–95	1995–96	1996–97
Central government expenditure[2]	167 636	175 700	179 600	183 200	187 200	1 700	−1 500	−2 300
Local authority expenditure[3]	69 305	73 400	73 400	74 700	75 800	1 400	−500	−1 100
Financing requirements of nationalised industries	4 447	1 520	−370	−360	80	180	−870	−290
Reserve			3 000	6 000	9 000	−3 500	−4 000	−4 500
Allowance for shortfall		−1 000				−1 000		
Control Total	**241 387**	**249 600**	**255 700**	**263 500**	**272 100**	**−1 300**	**−6 900**	**−8 300**
Cyclical social security	14 333	14 100	14 100	14 100	14 500	−700	−1 400	−2 100
Central government debt interest	19 223	22 100	24 500	26 000	26 200	−400	100	400
Accounting adjustments	8 020	9 500	10 700	12 500	12 700	200	200	900
General government expenditure excluding privatisation proceeds	**282 964**	**295 200**	**305 000**	**316 000**	**325 400**	**−2 100**	**−8 100**	**−9 100**
GGE excluding privatisation proceeds as a percent of GDP	44¼	43½	42½	41¾	41	−¼	−¾	−¾

[1] For definitions, rounding and other conventions, see notes in Annex A.
[2] Excluding cyclical social security.
[3] Comprises total central government support for local authorities and local authorities self-financed expenditure.

Real growth **6.11** Year on year, GGE is expected to grow by 0·1 per cent in real terms between 1994–95 and 1995–96, by 1·1 per cent in 1996–97, and by 0·7 per cent in 1997–98. These figures are also shown in Table 1.5. Average real growth over the three Survey years is 0·6 per cent, well within the projected growth rate of the economy.

6.12 Chart 6.4 shows the breakdown of GGE in 1993–94 by function. Further analysis of GGE for years up to 1994–95, by function and economic category, will be published early next year in the Statistical Supplement.

6 Public spending

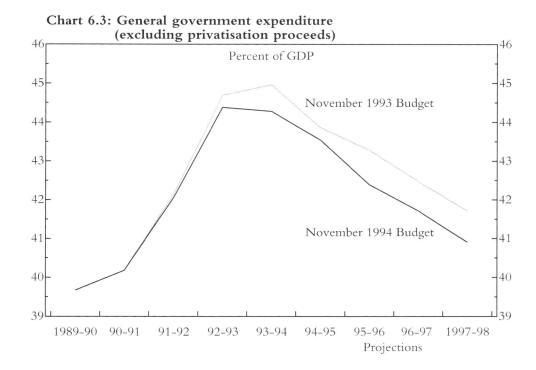

Chart 6.3: General government expenditure (excluding privatisation proceeds)

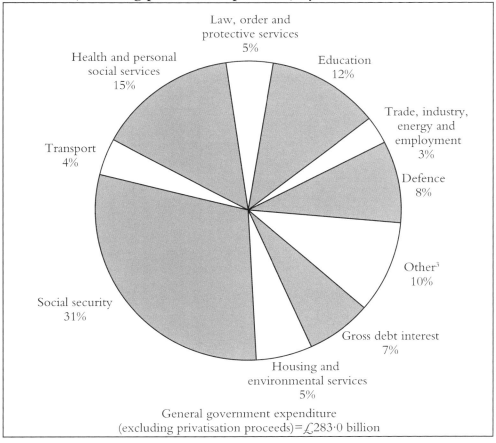

Chart 6.4: General government expenditure (excluding privatisation proceeds) by function in 1993-94[1,2]

General government expenditure (excluding privatisation proceeds) = £283·0 billion

[1] Spending in Scotland, Wales and Northern Ireland has been allocated to the appropriate functions.
[2] Local authority spending accounts for 24 per cent of the total.
[3] Includes national accounts adjustments.

Fundamental expenditure reviews

6.13 The programme of fundamental expenditure reviews, initiated in February 1993, has continued this year. These reviews have been considering long-term trends in spending, looking at ways in which services could be delivered more economically and effectively, and considering whether there are any areas from which the State should withdraw altogether. The results of these reviews have informed this year's decisions about spending priorities, and have contributed to some of the increases in efficiency reflected in the new plans.

6.14 The aim is to cover all departments of state in the course of the Parliament. The next batch of reviews will include the Department of National Heritage, the Ministry of Agriculture and other agriculture spending, the environmental programmes of the Department of the Environment and the Office of Public Service and Science.

Public sector pay and running costs

6.15 In line with the Chancellor's announcement on 14 September 1994, central government departments are expected to offset, or more than offset, pay and price increases through efficiencies and other economies. Budgetary provision for the rest of the public sector has been set on a comparable basis.

New plans **6.16** Provision for the running costs of civil departments, which was £15·0 billion in 1994–95, has been set at £14·8 billion in 1995–96, £14·7 billion in 1996–97 and £14·6 billion in 1997–98. Compared with previous plans, provision has been reduced by £300 million in 1995–96 and £500 million in 1996–97. The Ministry of Defence is no longer included in these figures, but provision for its operating costs is set on the same basis.

6 Public spending

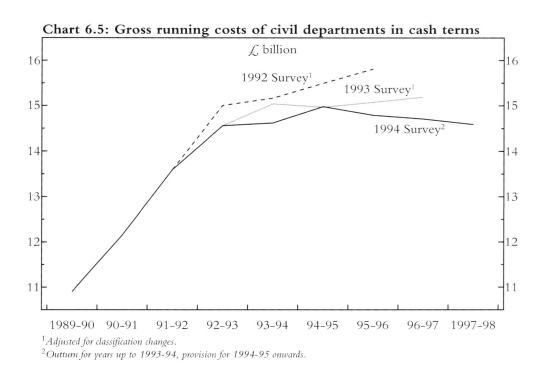

Chart 6.5: Gross running costs of civil departments in cash terms

[1] *Adjusted for classification changes.*
[2] *Outturn for years up to 1993-94, provision for 1994-95 onwards.*

6.17 As Chart 6.5 illustrates, the latest plans imply that running costs will be held broadly constant in cash terms over the four years from 1993–94 to 1997–98. In real terms, the plans imply a cut in running costs of 10 per cent over this period, as Chart 6.6 shows.

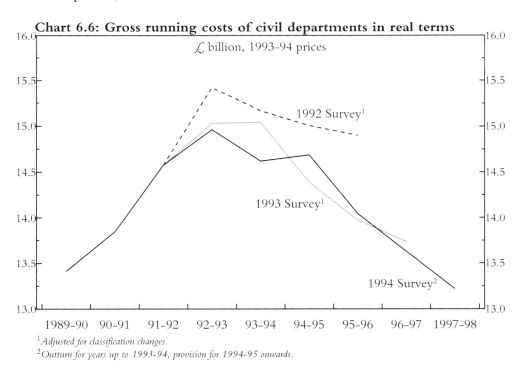

Chart 6.6: Gross running costs of civil departments in real terms

[1] *Adjusted for classification changes.*
[2] *Outturn for years up to 1993-94, provision for 1994-95 onwards.*

End year flexibility **6.18** Departments may now carry forward all underspends on running costs to add to provision in a later year. This allows them to manage their money sensibly from year to year. The underspend carried forward from 1993–94 totals £270 million.

6.19 The plans for running costs include extra resources for the Department of Social Security over the next two years to implement anti-fraud measures, the jobseeker's allowance and the new incapacity benefit. There are reductions in other departments as a result of lower unemployment and privatisations. Radical steps to reduce staff numbers have been announced by a number of departments, including Transport, Defence, Health and Customs and Excise.

Capital spending

6.20 Total public sector capital spending (measured net of receipts from asset sales) is expected to be £22·9 billion in 1994–95, up from £21·7 billion in 1993–94. The increase largely reflects the reprofiling of capital expenditure by local authorities. Details are set out in Table 6.4.

Table 6.4 Public sector capital expenditure[1]

	£ billion								
	Outturn					Estimated outturn	Projections		
	1989–90	1990–91	1991–92	1992–93	1993–94	1994–95	1995–96	1996–97	1997–98
Central government	7·7	9·6	10·3	10·9	9·9	9·1	8·8	9·3	9·4
Local authorities	6·9	5·9	7·0	6·9	6·5	8·0	6·9	6·7	6·5
Public corporations	5·6	5·2	4·3	5·3	5·3	5·8	6·2	5·3	5·0
Notional allocation of the Reserve							0·3	0·6	0·9
Total public sector capital expenditure	**20·3**	**20·7**	**21·6**	**23·1**	**21·7**	**22·9**	**22·2**	**22·0**	**21·8**
Less: Depreciation	11·7	10·9	9·9	10·1	10·1	10·3	10·3	10·4	10·7
Net public sector capital expenditure	**8·6**	**9·8**	**11·7**	**13·0**	**11·7**	**12·6**	**11·9**	**11·6**	**11·0**
Real terms (1993–94 prices) Gross of depreciation	24·9	23·6	23·1	23·8	21·7	22·5	21·0	20·4	19·7
Net of depreciation	10·5	11·2	12·5	13·4	11·7	12·4	11·3	10·7	10·0

[1] *Figures are shown for the national accounts definition of capital spending described in Annex A. They include the capital spending of industries now privatised, or planned to be privatised before 31 March 1998, while in the public sector.*

6.21 In 1995–96 public sector capital spending is expected to be £22·2 billion, implying a significant increase in real terms on the capital spending plans in last year's Budget. A large proportion of this is accounted for by higher spending by local authorities, who are now expected to carry forward significant unspent balances from the temporary relaxation of the rules governing the use of their capital receipts. The figures for 1996–97 and 1997–98 are boosted by projected capital expenditure of around £1 billion financed by the National Lottery, which though not part of the Control Total is included in GGE.

6 Public spending

6.22 The level of public sector capital spending beyond 1995–96 is particularly uncertain. After allowing for a conventional stylised allocation from the Reserve, capital spending is expected to remain broadly flat at around £22 billion.

6.23 However, direct spending by the public sector does not tell the whole story on capital spending. It takes no account of the impact of the private finance initiative.

Private finance   **6.24** The private finance initiative was launched in 1992 and the Private Finance Panel established under Sir Alastair Morton in November 1993. Significant progress has been achieved in attracting private sector capital into areas previously regarded as public, adding to overall capital spending. Around £500 million will have been invested by the end of 1994–95, and much more will follow.

6.25 For example, taking the four transport projects announced in the 1993 Budget: eleven consortia have now pre-qualified to bid for the first four design, build, finance and operate roads; the competition has been launched for the Docklands Light Railway Lewisham Extension; the Civil Aviation Authority hope very shortly to be going out to competition for the new Scottish Air Traffic Control Centre; and the specification study for the West Coast Main Line refurbishment will be finished by the end of the year. In addition, London Underground have been holding a competition for the provision of a privately financed Northern Line train service; bids are due back in from the four pre-qualified consortia on the Channel Tunnel Rail Link (CTRL) by March 1995; and the CTRL hybrid Bill was introduced in Parliament on 23 November.

6.26 Over 50 projects have been completed or approved which will bring in over £100 million of capital to the NHS.

6.27 Tenders have been received for the first two privately financed prisons, providing 1,400 places in Merseyside and South Wales. Contracts will be awarded by April 1995 with the prisons planned to open by 1997–98. Invitations to tender for the first secure training centre for juvenile offenders will be issued shortly.

6.28 Around £1 billion of information technology projects are currently going down or considering the private finance route. For example three bidders have been shortlisted to provide a replacement for the National Insurance Recording System, with preliminary bids to be received by the end of the year; and prequalification is under way for the project to automate post office counters.

6.29 Overall the Government expects to let contracts under the private finance initiative next year leading to around £5 billion of capital investment.

6.30 As well as building on initial successes, the private finance initiative is developing into new areas. For example, London Underground will be considering how to extend private finance into other areas of its business. Key candidates include power supplies and communications. Highland Regional Council have launched competitions for privately financed sewerage treatment works at Fort William and Inverness. This is the start of a programme of private finance projects in the water and sewerage sector in Scotland and Northern Ireland potentially worth over £1 billion. The Department of Social Security will shortly be inviting private finance proposals for the redevelopment of its site at Longbenton in Newcastle. The Ministry of Agriculture, Fisheries and Food are considering using private finance for the provision of new office facilities at Crewe and Northallerton. The Home Office will be procuring two further prisons under the private finance initiative, and the Scottish Office are currently looking at the case for a privately financed prison in Scotland. The London Docklands Development Corporation has invited tenders to form a joint venture company with them to provide infrastructure for environmentally responsible and competitive energy supplies in the Royal Docks. In education, universities already get approaching one third of their income from private sources.

The new plans: summary

6.31 Savings have been found on most programmes to reflect lower inflation, tight control of administrative costs and increased efficiency. Resources have also been switched between programmes to reflect priorities. In particular, savings are expected from a major effort to combat social security fraud, and reforms of housing benefit and income support for mortgage interest. On the other hand, the plans provide for a larger real increase in health spending than planned last Budget, and also protect the Government's achievements on law and order and education. The science budget and the aid programme have benefited from additions to last year's plans.

6.32 Table 6.5 analyses the Control Total by department showing changes from previous plans. Central government support for local authorities and the financing requirements of nationalised industries have been attributed to the appropriate departments.

6.33 Spending by each department since 1989–90 is set out in Annex A, Table 6A.3 (cash terms) and Table 6A.4 (real terms).

Table 6.5 Control Total by department[1]

	£ million							
	Outturn	Estimated outturn	New plans			Changes from previous plans		
	1993–94	1994–95	1995–96	1996–97	1997–98	1994–95	1995–96	1996–97
Defence	22 757	22 510	21 720	21 920	22 320	−260	−300	−200
Foreign Office	1 276	1 440	1 160	1 160	1 180	310	−10	−10
Overseas Development	2 239	2 400	2 360	2 420	2 480	90	0	60
Agriculture, Fisheries and Food	2 881	2 660	3 020	3 000	2 960	−150	40	20
Trade and Industry	2 805	1 860	1 380	800	750	10	−10	−10
ECGD	−60	−70	−20	10	10	10	70	80
Employment	3 509	3 720	3 460	3 480	3 440	−10	−70	−40
Transport	5 993	6 100	4 390	4 450	5 080	300	−1 130	−860
DOE – Housing	7 734	7 350	6 900	6 910	6 930	−170	−770	−740
DOE – Environment	2 202	2 170	1 980	1 920	1 910	30	130	70
DOE – PH, PSA etc	−93	−130	−210	−220	−240	40	60	80
DOE – Local government[2]	29 362	29 900	30 290	30 900	30 870	−30	−550	−1 510
Home Office	5 962	6 260	6 410	6 420	6 570	0	−60	−60
Legal departments	2 418	2 650	2 800	2 880	2 880	−90	−90	−120
Education	9 806	10 530	10 960	11 230	11 240	40	−180	−250
National Heritage	975	980	1 000	960	920	10	10	−10
Health	29 829	31 750	32 960	33 270	34 120	20	10	0
Social security[3]	67 671	70 360	72 970	76 250	79 500	1 460	−50	−50
Scotland	13 559	14 200	14 410	14 570	14 680	0	−220	−350
Wales	6 302	6 580	6 770	6 870	6 920	−60	−130	−180
Northern Ireland[3]	7 086	7 490	7 720	7 880	8 020	100	−20	−70
Chancellor's departments	3 340	3 390	3 220	3 190	3 140	−40	−150	−210
Cabinet Office – OPSS	1 241	1 320	1 340	1 360	1 390	10	0	10
Cabinet Office – other, etc	1 233	1 200	1 120	1 130	1 160	0	−30	−70
European Communities	1 836	2 040	2 820	2 760	2 640	690	−70	−160
Local authority self-financed expenditure	9 525	11 900	11 800	12 000	12 200	1 000	700	800
Reserve			3 000	6 000	9 000	−3 500	−4 000	−4 500
Allowance for shortfall		−1 000				−1 000		
Control Total	**241 387**	**249 600**	**255 700**	**263 500**	**272 100**	**−1 300**	**−6 900**	**−8 300**

[1] For definitions, rounding and other conventions, see notes in Annex A. See Annex B for the composition of each departmental grouping.
[2] The entry for the Department of the Environment includes payments of Revenue Support Grant and National Non-Domestic Rates to English local authorities. These finance, at local authorities' discretion, a range of local services, including education, social services and other environmental services.
[3] Excluding cyclical social security.

6 Public spending

Departmental detail

6.34 The following paragraphs briefly describe the new plans for each department. They should be read alongside the tables: they do not repeat the information provided there. The departmental reports to be published during February and March 1995 will give more details.

Defence

6.35 As envisaged in last year's Budget, defence spending will continue to fall in real terms over the coming years. The Defence Costs Study (DCS) was successful in identifying substantial savings in the support area, while preserving the front line. The new plans accommodate the costs of military redundancies flowing from the DCS, and the enhancements to the front line announced by the Secretary of State for Defence in July.

Foreign and Commonwealth Office

6.36 The new plans reflect the importance that the Government attaches to diplomacy following the end of the Cold War, and to the Department's overseas political and commercial effort. Compared with the plans in last year's Budget, the real value of provision is 2 per cent higher in 1995–96, and 1½ per cent higher in 1996–97.

Overseas development

6.37 The UK has the sixth largest aid programme in the world and extra resources have been added to previous plans. The real value of provision is 2½ per cent higher in 1995–96 and almost 5 per cent higher in 1996–97 than planned in last year's Budget.

Agriculture, Fisheries and Food

6.38 The new plans for agriculture reflect an increase in the estimated cost of agricultural support in the UK under the Common Agricultural Policy, largely due to a lower than expected "green pound", which determines the rate at which CAP support prices set in ECU are converted into national currency. These additions are offset by savings on domestic spending, mainly reductions in running costs and capital grants.

Trade and Industry – programme spending

6.39 Provision for DTI programmes will be higher in real terms in 1995–96 and 1996–97 than the plans in last year's Budget. DTI programmes are being developed and strengthened in the light of the Competitiveness White Paper. Priority is being given to the development of Business Links and services delivered through them including support for exports, innovation and good management practice. Improvements in delivery of DTI services and value for money will be secured by greater involvement of the private sector.

Trade and Industry – nationalised industries

6.40 Provision is made for the external financing limits (EFLs) of Nuclear Electric, the Post Office and British Shipbuilders, and for meeting the cost of residual liabilities in the coal industry after privatisation. The plans for Nuclear Electric include the costs of a restructuring package in 1995–96 and 1996–97, which is expected to contribute to a significant increase in efficiency in 1997–98. Provision for the Post Office is held at the levels set in the last Budget. The plans for coal will allow offers to be made to buy out concessionary coal entitlements in 1997–98.

6 Public spending

Export Credits Guarantee Department

6.41 The department, through its Fixed Rate Export Finance programme, provides medium- to long-term fixed interest rate support at interest rates set by the OECD. Increases in plans reflect ECGD's exposure to movements in interest and exchange rates. To a limited extent they are offset by OECD agreement to cut interest rate subsidies and technical adjustments to the terms on offer.

Help for exporters

There will be a general review of the premiums paid by exporters for medium- or long-term ECGD cover which will lead to reductions, on average, of around 10 per cent. In addition, for a number of important developing markets, the cover provided in 1996–97 will be rolled forward and increased by £300 million, taking the total in 1997–98 to £3·5 billion. This cover does not count as public expenditure, nor against the PSBR, but could add to the PSBR in future if ECGD had to meet substantial claims.

Employment

6.42 The new Employment Department plans focus on helping unemployed people to get jobs in the context of the new jobseeker's allowance. There are net savings in both programme and running costs reflecting efficiency improvements and lower unemployment.

6.43 As part of the package described in the box on pages 124–125, a number of innovative schemes will be introduced or extended, including incentives to employers to recruit the long-term unemployed, work experience opportunities and targeted help with jobsearch.

6.44 There will be a major reform of the Training for Work programme aimed at increasing the number of trainees who move into jobs. The plans also provide for Modern Apprenticeships and the new training measures announced in the Competitiveness White Paper.

Transport

6.45 The new plans for transport reflect the decision to reduce national roads expenditure compared with previous plans. Central government support for spending on local roads and transport will also be reduced. But substantial spending to maintain and improve trunk roads and motorways in England will continue: with over £5 billion planned for the next three years. Over the next three years it is also expected that substantial private finance will be introduced, with the first four contracts for private sector firms to design, build, finance and operate trunk roads due to be negotiated by the middle of next year. This will help to minimise the impact of the reduction in provision on the trunk road programme.

Transport – Nationalised Industries

6.46 The department's programmes also include the financing of railways, together with the external financing limits of London Transport and the Civil Aviation Authority (CAA). Total funding for the core activities of the railways (British Rail, Railtrack, Union Railways and European Passenger Services) remains unchanged from previous plans in 1995–96. Other changes in financial provision for railways over the next three financial years reflect the effects of privatisation.

6.47 Investment in London Transport should be around £1 billion in 1995–96, including considerable support for the Jubilee Line Extension and the Crossrail project, as well as a substantial order under the private finance initiative for the provision of a new Northern Line train service. CAA plans have been reduced over the period since there is further potential to attract private finance for their investment.

DOE – Housing, Environment and PSA Services

6.48 The new plans incorporate a reduction in the Housing Corporation capital provision, which will now be at a level of around £1·35 billion a year. There are substantial estimating savings on housing benefit for local authority tenants, reflecting the lower inflation forecast and a reduction in the number of tenants expected to need assistance. The reduced Housing Revenue Account subsidy provision also reflects changes in housing benefit policy and the consequential savings from an increasing effort by DSS and local authorities to combat benefit fraud. Local authority credit approvals for housing renovation have been reduced. An extra £30 million is being provided over three years for the Home Energy Efficiency scheme.

6.49 Within the Single Regeneration Budget, created last year, more than £800 million is being made available for new regeneration projects. This will provide extra resources for the first bidding round and for the launch of a second bidding round with funding beginning in 1996–97.

Home Office

6.50 Law and order continues to be a key Government priority. The new plans include sufficient provision to sustain police numbers, taking account of the savings to come from the Sheehy reforms. The plans also make provision for 4,000 extra prison places, and allow for increased expenditure on security and safety measures. Additional resources have also been found to increase the effectiveness of immigration control, and to deal with increased asylum applications.

Legal departments

6.51 Provision for these departments is slightly lower in real terms than the plans in the last Budget. These savings come from increased efficiency, savings in lower priority areas of programmes, and continuing tight control of legal aid spending. Legal services including legal aid were subject to a fundamental expenditure review this year. Any major changes flowing from this will be subject to public consultation, likely to be in the New Year.

6 Public spending

Education **6.52** Total education spending by central government in England (including support for local authorities) will rise in real terms, to almost £11 billion in 1995–96. The new plans will allow almost one in three young people to enter higher education and maintain in real terms the support available for students from loans and maintenance grants. The new plans provide for continued expansion of student numbers in further education and further growth in the number of grant-maintained schools.

National Heritage **6.53** The plans for the Department of National Heritage allow extra money in 1995–96 for the new British Library and the celebrations for VE and VJ Day. The plans for later years reflect lower inflation and scope for efficiency savings in future. The Department will be undertaking a fundamental expenditure review to be completed in 1995.

6.54 The National Lottery will bring in considerable extra money for spending on a wide range of sporting and cultural projects (perhaps giving them as much as £1 billion every year once it is well established) in addition to the Government's existing spending. Spending of lottery money counts as general government expenditure, but is outside the Control Total.

Health **6.55** The priority the Government attaches to spending on the NHS is illustrated by spending plans that continue to increase significantly in real terms year by year, more than fulfilling its manifesto commitment. Planned spending on the NHS in England in 1995–96 is £32·0 billion, £1·3 billion higher than the 1994–95 plans and representing real growth of 1 per cent. This increase comes on top of real growth in 1994–95 plans over 1993–94 outturn of 3·8 per cent.

6.56 At the same time, the NHS will benefit from an improvement in efficiency in 1995–96 of at least 3 per cent, equivalent to an additional £600 million in 1995–96 for patient care. Initiatives to scale back bureaucracy will save approaching £200 million a year by 1997-98, which will be ploughed back into the NHS in full. This combination of extra resources and improved efficiency, with pay rises being financed through efficiency growth, will increase the number of patients treated in 1995-96 by around 4 per cent. Private finance will also add significantly to the total resources devoted to the NHS in 1995–96.

Social Security **6.57** The new social security plans incorporate revised estimates of the number of claimants and provide for the uprating of benefits over the coming years. The assumptions used for benefit upratings, and for unemployment are set out in Annex A to Chapter 3. In addition, the plans include the extra help in pensions and income related benefits following the introduction of VAT on domestic fuel and power.

Work incentives

The Budget includes a package of new measures costing £680 million in 1996–97, of which £375 million is public expenditure, to help unemployed people back to work and reduce the cost to employers of taking on the unemployed.

Four measures to encourage employers to take on the unemployed

- Employers' **national insurance contributions** will be cut by 0·6 per cent for people earning less than £205 a week from April 1995.

- Employers who hire someone who has been been out of work for two years or more will be able to get a full **NIC rebate** for that person for up to one year, starting in April 1996.

- The **Work Trials** scheme is being expanded. This enables employers to give people who have been out of work for over six months a three week trial in a job before deciding whether to take them on permanently. During the trial the unemployed continue to receive their benefits, so the scheme is free to employers. Work Trials will offer 150,000 places over the next three years.

- Further **Workstart** pilot schemes will be developed, giving incentives to employers to recruit the long term unemployed, and helping about 5,000 people. The details of the pilots are being finalised.

Four measures to ease the transition from unemployment to work

- People who have been out of work for at least six months will be able to get their **housing benefit** and **council tax benefit** paid at their full existing rates for the first four weeks after they take a job, from April 1996. The aim will be to ensure that, within the four weeks, people will be told how much continuing help they will get with their rent and council tax, and that this will be paid promptly.

- **Family credit** will be paid more quickly. The aim is to ensure that by April 1996, 95 per cent of new claims from employees will be dealt with within five working days of the Department of Social Security receiving the claim.

6.58 The new plans also reflect the reform of benefits for the unemployed, to create the new jobseeker's allowance, for which legislation will be enacted in the 1994–95 Parliamentary session. They include savings from a proposed reform of housing benefit, so as to give tenants and landlords incentives to economise on rents, to limit housing benefit payments on empty property, and increases in the contributions made by non dependant members of households in assessing housing benefit. Some of the costs of the work incentives measures (see box above) also fall on social security within the Control Total.

6.59 The plans also take account of the administrative costs of an intensified effort to combat benefit fraud: some of the savings are scored within the Control Total, although the bulk are reflected in lower estimates of cyclical social security – see paragraphs 6.72 and 6.73 below.

- People who lose benefit because they do some work while on income support or the new jobseeker's allowance will qualify for a lump sum of up to £1,000 when they leave those benefits to start work of 16 hours or more. This **Back-to-Work Bonus** will be tax-free.

- There will be more help with initial work expenses for people who have been out of work for at least two years, through the **Jobfinder's Grant**, which is being extended nationally. Around 25,000 grants will be available each year, worth an average £200 each.

Two measures to help people who want full-time work

- Anyone eligible for family credit who works 30 hours or more will get a **full timer's premium** of an extra £10 a week from July 1995. Changes to housing benefit and council tax benefit will be made to ensure that people who also qualify for these benefits gain by the full £10.

- There will be further **Jobmatch** pilots with up to 3,000 places to help the long-term unemployed build up full-time hours and wages by combining a number of part-time jobs.

Three measures to keep the unemployed in touch with the labour market

- **1-2-1** interviews and **Workwise** courses, providing intensive help in how to look for work, will be extended nationally for 18 to 24 year olds unemployed for over a year who refuse other offers of help.

- **Community Action** will provide work experience and increase help in how to look for work for people who have been unemployed for a year or more. About 40,000 people will benefit each year.

Trying out new ways to help the unemployed without children

- A **new in-work benefit** for childless couples and single people, based on family credit, will be piloted for three years from October 1996, to see how effective it will be.

Scotland, Wales and Northern Ireland

6.60 Changes in these programmes reflect in the main the effect of changes in comparable programmes in England. Each Secretary of State has wide discretion about the distribution of expenditure within his programme; detailed plans will be announced shortly.

Chancellor's departments

6.61 The expenditure of the Chancellor's departments is very largely accounted for by the Inland Revenue and Customs and Excise, and is taken up mainly by running costs. Fundamental expenditure reviews have been undertaken by these two departments and also the Treasury this year. Some of the resulting efficiency savings are reflected in these new spending plans.

Office of Public Service and Science

6.62 Extra resources have been provided for basic and strategic scientific research so that it will be maintained in real terms in 1995–96 at this year's record level.

Science and technology

6.63 Total central government spending on science and technology in 1995–96 will be about £6·1 billion, broadly in line with previous plans.

European Community

6.64 Compared with the previous forecast, net payments are higher in 1994–95, but slightly lower thereafter. The uneven profile arises because contributions are paid on the basis of agreed estimates of contributions likely to be due, which are subsequently adjusted in the light of later information. The main reason for the higher forecast of net payments in 1994–95 is that the amount of contributions which was brought forward within the 1994 European Union budgetary year to reflect the timing of reimbursements of CAP expenditure to Member States was much lower than anticipated.

6.65 In the later years, the forecast continues to reflect the decisions taken at the Edinburgh European Council in December 1992, and the United Kingdom's growth relative to other Member States.

Local authorities

6.66 Local authority spending is financed by support provided by central government and from local authorities' own resources. Table 6.6 summarises the projections of local authority spending, showing the new plans for central government support and projected local authority self-financed expenditure.

6.67 The level of local authority spending is determined by individual authorities, taking account of support provided by central government, finance available from their own resources and their decisions on local taxation. The Government intends to use its powers to cap local authority budgets, should that prove necessary.

6.68 For 1995–96, Total Standard Spending (TSS) in England – ie the amount which the Government thinks it is appropriate for local authorities to spend on revenue expenditure – has been set at £43·5 billion, after transfers. For 1996–97 and 1997–98, TSS has been set at £44·1 billion and £44·6 billion respectively. These figures include provision for care in the community. Adjusting for functional change, the increase next year over 1994–95 is 0·9 per cent excluding community care, and 2·2 per cent including it.

6.69 Central support for local authorities' revenue expenditure in 1995–96, Aggregate External Finance (AEF), has been set at £42·4 billion for Great Britain as a whole.

6.70 Gross capital expenditure by local authorities in 1995–96 is expected to be £8¾ billion, somewhat lower than the levels in 1993–94 and 1994–95, which were boosted by the temporary relaxation of the capital receipts rules announced in the 1992 Autumn Statement. Capital receipts in 1995–96 are projected to be around £3¼ billion, giving net capital spending of around £5¾ billion.

6 Public spending

Other public expenditure   **6.71** In addition to expenditure within the Control Total, GGE also includes cyclical social security, privatisation proceeds, and debt interest.

Cyclical social security   **6.72** Cyclical social security is defined as unemployment benefit and income support paid to people of working age. The forecast for cyclical social security show substantial reductions compared with those in the last Budget reflecting the improved prospects for inflation and unemployment (the detail of the assumptions underlying the plans are set out in Annex A of Chapter 3.

6.73 There are also measures which reduce cyclical social security by £0·4 billion in 1995–96 and £0·7 billion in 1996–97 and by £0·9 billion in 1997–98. The bulk of this is the savings expected to flow from the anti-fraud initiative referred to in paragraph 6.59 above, and the savings in Income Support following the Government's decision to place limits on the amount of assistance made available for mortgage interest payments. These figures also include some of the costs of the work incentives measures described in the box on pages 124-125.

Accounting adjustments   **6.74** The accounting adjustments include various other items within general government expenditure but outside the Control Total. The increase between 1994–95 and 1996–97 mainly reflects expenditure of the proceeds of the National Lottery and the effects of early retirements on civil and armed forces superannuation payments.

Privatisation proceeds   **6.75** Privatisation proceeds are projected to be £3 billion in 1995–96, £3 billion in 1996–97 and £2 billion in 1997–98.

Debt interest   **6.76** General government gross debt interest is projected to rise from £19·7 billion in 1993–94 to £26·6 billion in 1997–98. Gross debt interest payments declined from 5¼ per cent of GDP in 1981–82 to just over 3 per cent in 1993–94. Debt interest payments are projected to rise to 3½ per cent in 1995–96 and 1996–97, then fall back to 3¼ per cent in 1997–98. Table 6A.6 in Annex A shows the total for gross and net general government debt interest.

6 Public spending

Table 6.6 Local authority expenditure[1]

	£ million							
	Outturn	Estimated outturn	New plans			Changes from previous plans		
	1993-94	1994-95	1995-96	1996-97	1997-98	1994-95	1995-96	1996-97
Current								
Aggregate External Finance[2,3]								
England	33 229	34 330	34 670	34 810	34 860	20	−650	−1 500
Scotland[4]	5 214	5 310	5 310	5 340	5 300	30	−70	−160
Wales[4]	2 338	2 420	2 450	2 450	2 430	0	−40	−110
Total Aggregate External Finance	**40 781**	**42 070**	**42 440**	**42 590**	**42 600**	**60**	**−770**	**−1 760**
Other current grants	13 116	13 750	13 800	14 630	15 590	380	−330	−60
Total current support	**53 898**	**55 820**	**56 230**	**57 220**	**58 200**	**430**	**−1 100**	**−1 820**
Capital[2]								
Capital grants	1 801	1 600	1 510	1 550	1 580	60	−100	−10
Credit approvals	4 082	4 010	3 940	3 950	3 820	−10	30	−90
Total capital support	**5 883**	**5 610**	**5 450**	**5 490**	**5 400**	**50**	**−70**	**−90**
Total central government support to local authorities	**59 780**	**61 400**	**61 700**	**62 700**	**63 600**	**500**	**−1 200**	**−1 900**
Local authority self-financed expenditure	**9 525**	**11 900**	**11 800**	**12 000**	**12 200**	**1 000**	**700**	**800**
Total local authority expenditure	**69 305**	**73 400**	**73 400**	**74 700**	**75 800**	**1 400**	**−500**	**−1 100**

[1] For definitions, rounding and other conventions, see Annex A.
[2] Provision for local government re-organisation is included in capital support whereas last year it scored in AEF.
[3] Aggregate External Finance includes Revenue Support Grant, distribution of Non-domestic Rate Revenue and a number of specific grants which fund part of the expenditure on a specific service or activity.
[4] Scottish and Welsh figures for 1996–97 and 1997–98 are illustrative; final figures will depend on the Secretary of State's decisions on the allocation of resources.

Annex A to Chapter 6
Public Expenditure Analyses

This annex includes a number of more detailed analyses of expenditure. It also explains the conventions used in presenting the figures throughout Chapter 6.

Rounding conventions **6A.1** For tables presenting the new plans the following conventions apply:

Future years: Departments' spending totals within the Control Total are rounded to the nearest £10 million (except for non-cyclical social security in 1996–97 and 1997–98, which is rounded to £50 million). The Control Total and spending sector totals (except financing requirements of the nationalised industries), items outside the Control Total, and projections of capital spending are rounded to the nearest £100 million.

1994–95: The rounding conventions adopted for future years also apply to figures for 1994–95, to reflect their provisional nature.

6A.2 For tables which show the Control Total and GGE in real terms, all figures are rounded to the nearest £100 million. Projections of capital spending in real terms are also rounded to the nearest £100 million.

6A.3 Changes and totals in the tables are based on unrounded figures. They may therefore differ from the changes and sums of the rounded figures.

6A.4 Some figures may be subject to detailed amendment before the publication of the Statistical Supplement early in 1995.

Calculation of changes previous plans and projections **6A.5** Changes from previous plans are differences from the plans and projections for 1994–95 to 1996–97 in the February 1994 Statistical Supplement after account is taken of classification changes and transfers and switches between departments.

6A.6 The most significant such item included in this Report is a switch from the Ministry of Defence and the Foreign Office to the Cabinet Office as a result of the creation of a single intelligence Vote.

6A.7 There is only one material classification change affecting the aggregate figures. Reflecting the changed national accounting treatment introduced in the 1994 "Blue Book", British Nuclear Fuels Limited is treated from 1992–93 as a public corporation. This classification change also affects the PSBR. There are a few minor classification changes but none which affect the Control Total by more than £25 million in any year: none of these affects the PSBR.

Real terms figures **6A.8** Figures in real terms are cash levels adjusted to 1993–94 price levels by excluding the effects of general inflation as measured by the GDP deflator. The deflator series used is adjusted to remove the distortion caused by the abolition of domestic rates. A description of the method of adjustment was set out in Annex C to Chapter 1 of the 1990 Autumn Statement.

Annex A to Chapter 6: Public expenditure analyses

Measurement of capital spending 6A.9 The main analysis set out in Table 6.4 shows the expenditure components of the public sector's capital account, on national accounting definitions, measured net of estimated depreciation. The figures include:

(i) gross domestic fixed capital formation, ie expenditure on fixed assets – schools, hospitals, roads, computers, plant and machinery etc. This is measured net of receipts from sales of fixed assets (eg council houses and surplus land);

(ii) grants in support of capital spending by the private sector;

(iii) the value of the physical increase in stocks (for central government, primarily agricultural commodity stocks); less

(iv) estimates of depreciation on the public sector's stock of fixed assets. These are based on the national accounts series produced by the Central Statistical Office (eg in Table 14.3 of the Blue Book), together with projections by the Treasury.

Central government expenditure 6A.10 This includes the financing requirements of trading funds and public corporations other than the nationalised industries. Cyclical social security spending is excluded from the measure of central government spending within the Control Total.

Central government support for local authorities 6A.11 This includes such items as mandatory student awards and community charge benefit which are administered by local authorities but all or most of the cost of which is paid by central government.

Local authority self-financed expenditure 6A.12 Local authority self-financed expenditure is the difference between total local authority expenditure, including debt interest but net of capital receipts, and central government support to local authorities.

Allowance for shortfall 6A.13 Tables setting out the estimated outturn for the Control Total in 1994–95 include an allowance for the difference between the overall assessment of likely outturn and the sum of the other components shown.

Adjustments 6A.14 The accounting adjustments include various items within general government expenditure but outside the Control Total (other than central government debt interest and cyclical social security, which are shown separately). The larger items are non-trading capital consumption, refunds of VAT, teachers' and NHS pensions increase payments, the difference between civil service and armed forces pensions payments and accruing superannuation liability charges, the debt remuneration element of NHS Trusts' charges to health authorities, and the spending of the proceeds of the National Lottery. The net market and overseas borrowing of nationalised industries and other public corporations is on the other hand within the Control Total but outside general government expenditure such that net repayments add to the magnitude of the accounting adjustments. Debt interest paid from local authorities to central government reduces the accounting adjustments. This is removed to avoid double counting between local government debt interest payments (which are shown inside local authority expenditure) and central government debt interest. Fuller details of the national accounting adjustments are given in the Statistical Supplement.

Table 6A.1 Public expenditure, 1963–64 to 1997–98

	Control Total[1]		General government expenditure (excluding privatisation proceeds)			Privatisation proceeds	General government expenditure	Money GDP[2]		Adjusted GDP deflator
	£ billion	Real terms[3] £ billion	£ billion	Real terms[3] £ billion	Percent of GDP[2]	£ billion	£ billion	£ billion	Adjusted series, Index (1990-91 =100)	Index (1993-94 =100)
1963–64			11·3	123·8	36¾		11·3	31·4	5·5	9·2
1964–65			12·3	128·1	36½		12·3	34·2	6·0	9·6
1965–66			13·6	135·7	37¾		13·6	36·6	6·5	10·0
1966–67			15·1	144·1	39½		15·1	38·9	6·9	10·4
1967–68			17·5	162·4	43¼		17·5	41·2	7·3	10·7
1968–69			18·2	161·6	41½		18·2	44·6	7·9	11·3
1969–70			19·3	162·7	41		19·3	48·0	8·5	11·9
1970–71			21·6	168·0	41¼		21·6	53·2	9·4	12·9
1971–72			24·4	173·6	41¾		24·4	59·3	10·5	14·0
1972–73			27·6	182·1	41½		27·6	67·6	11·9	15·2
1973–74			32·0	197·1	43½		32·0	75·0	13·2	16·2
1974–75			42·9	220·9	48¾		42·9	89·4	15·8	19·4
1975–76			53·8	221·1	49¼		53·8	111·2	19·6	24·3
1976–77			59·6	215·7	46¾		59·6	130·0	22·9	27·6
1977–78			64·4	205·2	43¼	−0·5	63·9	151·3	26·7	31·4
1978–79			75·0	214·9	44		75·0	173·7	30·6	34·9
1979–80			90·4	221·9	44	−0·4	90·0	208·6	36·8	40·7
1980–81			108·8	225·9	46½	−0·2	108·6	237·7	41·9	48·2
1981–82			121·0	228·9	47¼	−0·5	120·5	261·0	46·0	52·9
1982–83			133·1	235·1	47½	−0·5	132·7	285·8	50·4	56·6
1983–84			141·6	239·0	46½	−1·1	140·4	310·0	54·7	59·2
1984–85	126·0	202·6	152·8	245·6	46¾	−2·0	150·8	332·1	58·6	62·2
1985–86	129·6	197·4	161·2	245·6	45	−2·7	158·5	364·9	64·4	65·6
1986–87	136·0	201·2	169·3	250·4	44	−4·5	164·8	392·7	69·3	67·6
1987–88	148·6	208·7	178·4	250·5	41¾	−5·1	173·2	434·8	76·7	71·2
1988–89	156·1	205·4	186·9	245·9	39¼	−7·1	179·8	484·1	85·4	76·0
1989–90	175·1	215·4	205·0	252·3	39¾	−4·2	200·8	525·8	92·9	81·3
1990–91	193·4	220·2	223·5	254·5	40¼	−5·3	218·1	556·8	100·0	87·8
1991–92	212·5	227·7	244·2	261·7	42	−7·9	236·3	580·8		93·3
1992–93	231·3	238·3	268·4	276·6	44½	−8·2	260·2	604·8		97·0
1993–94	241·4	241·4	283·0	283·0	44¼	−5·4	277·5	639·0		100·0
1994–95	249·6	244·7	295·2	289·4	43½	−6·3	288·9	678		102·0
1995–96	255·7	242·8	305·0	289·6	42½	−3·0	302·0	720		105·3
1996–97	263·5	244·1	316·0	292·8	41¾	−3·0	313·0	758		107·9
1997–98	272·1	246·5	325·4	294·8	41	−2·0	323·4	796		110·4

[1] *Figures for the Control Total are only available on a consistent basis for the years shown. Figures are estimated outturn for 1994–95 and plans for 1995–96 onwards.*

[2] *An adjusted series for money GDP is used in the calculation of the ratio for years up to 1989–90. This has been constructed to remove the distortion caused by the abolition of domestic rates. A description of the adjustment method was given in Annex C to Chapter 1 of the 1990 Autumn Statement. The adjusted series is shown here as an index, based on the level of money GDP in 1990–91. For 1990–91 onwards the adjusted figure is identical to the figures shown for money GDP. For any earlier year the adjusted GDP figures can be calculated by applying the index level relevant for the year in question to the level of money GDP in 1990–91.*

[3] *Cash figures adjusted to price levels of 1993–94.*

Table 6A.2 General government expenditure (excluding privatisation proceeds): plans and outturn[1]

Percent of GDP

	1989–90	1990–91	1991–92	1992–93	1993–94	1994–95	1995–96	1996–97	1997–98
January 1990 White Paper (Cm 1021)	**39½**	40	39¾	39½					
February 1991 Supplement (Cm 1520)	**39½**	**40**	39¾	39¾	39¼				
February 1992 Supplement (Cm 1920)	**40**	**40**	**41¾**	42	42	41½			
January 1993 Supplement (Cm 2219)	**39¾**	**40¼**	**42¼**	**45**	45¼	45	44¼		
February 1994 Supplement (Cm 2519)	**39¾**	**40¼**	**42¼**	**44¾**	**45**	43¾	43¼	42½	
This Budget	**39¾**	**40¼**	**42**	**44½**	**44¼**	**43½**[2]	42½	41¾	41

Plans
Outturn

[1] *To avoid the distortion caused by the abolition of domestic rates, the ratios for years before 1990–91 are based on the adjusted series for money GDP (see footnote 2 to Table 6A.1). The figures from earlier publications are based on the figures underlying those publications, but the GDP figures on which they were based have been similarly adjusted. Figures for GGE in previous publications have been adjusted for classification changes.*

[2] *Estimated*

Annex A to Chapter 6: Public expenditure analyses

Table 6A.3 Control Total by department[1]

£ million

	Outturn					Estimated outturn	New plans			Changes from previous plans		
	1989–90	1990–91	1991–92	1992–93	1993–94	1994–95	1995–96	1996–97	1997–98	1994–95	1995–96	1996–97
Defence	20 777	21 709	22 913	22 910	22 757	22 510	21 720	21 920	22 320	-260	-300	-200
Foreign Office	898	968	1 132	1 278	1 276	1 440	1 160	1 160	1 180	310	-10	-10
Overseas Development	1 688	1 738	1 993	2 143	2 239	2 400	2 360	2 420	2 480	90	0	60
Agriculture, Fisheries and Food	1 487	2 137	2 159	2 198	2 881	2 660	3 020	3 000	2 960	-150	40	20
Trade and Industry	1 615	3 506	3 143	2 668	2 805	1 860	1 380	800	750	10	-10	-10
ECGD	358	372	215	117	-60	-70	-20	10	10	10	70	80
Employment	3 579	3 643	3 467	3 482	3 509	3 720	3 460	3 480	3 440	-10	-70	-40
Transport	3 562	4 682	5 363	6 601	5 993	6 100	4 390	4 450	5 080	300	-1 130	-860
DOE – Housing	2 938	6 742	7 493	8 232	7 734	7 350	6 900	6 910	6 930	-170	-770	-740
DOE – Environment	1 412	1 667	1 791	2 203	2 202	2 170	1 980	1 920	1 910	30	130	70
DOE – PH, PSA etc	-56	-31	-86	-198	-93	-130	-210	-220	-240	40	60	80
DOE – Local government	19 534	20 396	28 180	30 993	29 362	29 900	30 290	30 900	30 870	-30	-550	-1 510
Home Office	4 077	4 839	5 517	5 821	5 962	6 260	6 410	6 420	6 570	0	-60	-60
Legal departments	1 376	1 638	2 000	2 331	2 418	2 650	2 800	2 880	2 880	-90	-90	-120
Education	4 866	5 656	6 336	7 124	9 806	10 530	10 960	11 230	11 240	40	-180	-250
National Heritage	709	778	883	1 004	975	980	1 000	960	920	10	10	-10
Health	20 004	22 524	25 658	28 267	29 829	31 750	32 960	33 270	34 120	20	10	0
Social Security[2]	45 999	48 926	54 975	61 794	67 671	70 360	72 970	76 250	79 500	1 460	-50	-50
Scotland	8 948	9 717	11 697	12 713	13 559	14 200	14 410	14 570	14 680	0	-220	-350
Wales	3 801	4 442	5 309	5 992	6 302	6 580	6 770	6 870	6 920	-60	-130	-180
Northern Ireland[2]	5 395	5 525	6 018	6 580	7 086	7 490	7 720	7 880	8 020	100	-20	-70
Chancellor's departments	3 152	3 344	3 392	3 429	3 340	3 390	3 220	3 190	3 140	-40	-150	-210
Cabinet Office – OPSS	892	977	1 044	1 108	1 241	1 320	1 340	1 360	1 390	10	0	10
Cabinet Office – other, etc	274	313	363	1 123	1 233	1 200	1 120	1 130	1 160	0	-30	-70
European Communities	2 316	2 027	705	1 898	1 836	2 040	2 820	2 760	2 640	690	-70	-160
Local authority self-financed expenditure	15 518	15 120	10 843	9 448	9 525	11 900	11 800	12 000	12 200	1 000	700	800
Reserve							3 000	6 000	9 000	-3 500	-4 000	-4 500
Allowance for shortfall						-1 000				-1 000		
Control Total	**175 118**	**193 354**	**212 504**	**231 258**	**241 387**	**249 600**	**255 700**	**263 500**	**272 100**	**-1 300**	**-6 900**	**-8 300**

[1] For definitions, rounding and other conventions, see notes on page 129. See Annex B for the composition of each departmental grouping.
[2] Excluding cyclical social security.

Annex A to Chapter 6: Public expenditure analyses

Table 6A.4 Control Total by department in real terms[1]

£ billion

	Outturn					Estimated Outturn	New plans		
	1989–90	1990–91	1991–92	1992–93	1993–94	1994–95	1995–96	1996–97	1997–98
Defence	25·6	24·7	24·6	23·6	22·8	22·1	20·6	20·3	20·2
Foreign Office	1·1	1·1	1·2	1·3	1·3	1·4	1·1	1·1	1·1
Overseas Development	2·1	2·0	2·1	2·2	2·2	2·3	2·2	2·2	2·2
Agriculture, Fisheries and Food	1·8	2·4	2·3	2·3	2·9	2·6	2·9	2·8	2·7
Trade and Industry	2·0	4·0	3·4	2·7	2·8	1·8	1·3	0·7	0·7
ECGD	0·4	0·4	0·2	0·1	-0·1	-0·1	0·0	0·0	0·0
Employment	4·4	4·1	3·7	3·6	3·5	3·6	3·3	3·2	3·1
Transport	4·4	5·3	5·7	6·8	6·0	6·0	4·2	4·1	4·6
DOE – Housing	3·6	7·7	8·0	8·5	7·7	7·2	6·5	6·4	6·3
DOE – Environment	1·7	1·9	1·9	2·3	2·2	2·1	1·9	1·8	1·7
DOE – PH, PSA etc	-0·1	0·0	-0·1	-0·2	-0·1	-0·1	-0·2	-0·2	-0·2
DOE – Local government	24·0	23·2	30·2	31·9	29·4	29·3	28·8	28·6	28·0
Home Office	5·0	5·5	5·9	6·0	6·0	6·1	6·1	5·9	5·9
Legal departments	1·7	1·9	2·1	2·4	2·4	2·6	2·7	2·7	2·6
Education	6·0	6·4	6·8	7·3	9·8	10·3	10·4	10·4	10·2
National Heritage	0·9	0·9	0·9	1·0	1·0	1·0	1·0	0·9	0·8
Health	24·6	25·7	27·5	29·1	29·8	31·1	31·3	30·8	30·9
Social Security[2]	56·6	55·7	58·9	63·7	67·7	69·0	69·3	70·6	72·0
Scotland	11·0	11·1	12·5	13·1	13·6	13·9	13·7	13·5	13·3
Wales	4·7	5·1	5·7	6·2	6·3	6·5	6·4	6·4	6·3
Northern Ireland[2]	6·6	6·3	6·4	6·8	7·1	7·3	7·3	7·3	7·3
Chancellor's departments	3·9	3·8	3·6	3·5	3·3	3·3	3·1	3·0	2·8
Cabinet Office – OPSS	1·1	1·1	1·1	1·1	1·2	1·3	1·3	1·3	1·3
Cabinet Office – other, etc	0·3	0·4	0·4	1·2	1·2	1·2	1·1	1·0	1·0
European Communities	2·8	2·3	0·8	2·0	1·8	2·0	2·7	2·6	2·4
Local authority self-financed expenditure	19·1	17·2	11·6	9·7	9·5	11·7	11·2	11·1	11·0
Reserve							2·8	5·6	8·2
Allowance for shortfall						-1·0			
Control Total	**215·4**	**220·2**	**227·7**	**238·3**	**241·4**	**244·7**	**242·8**	**244·1**	**246·5**

[1] 1993–94 prices. For definitions, rounding and other conventions, see notes on page 129. See Annex B for the composition of each departmental grouping.
[2] Excluding cyclical social security.

Annex A to Chapter 6: Public expenditure analyses

Table 6A.5 Financing requirements of the nationalised industries, by department and industry[1]

£ million

	Outturn					Estimated outturn	New plans			Changes from previous plans		
	1989–90	1990–91	1991–92	1992–93	1993–94	1994–95	1995–96	1996–97	1997–98	1994–95	1995–96	1996–97
Trade and Industry	**17**	**1 903**	**1 702**	**1 679**	**2 125**	**1 000**	**440**	**50**	**–320**	**50**	**–30**	**0**
British Coal[2]	1 292	890	605	778	1 592	740	380	340	310	40	–80	0
British Shipbuilders	4	28	–9	–10	–9	10	0	0	0	10	0	0
Electricity (England and Wales)[3]	–1 262	985	1 180	991	726	480	270	–110	–450	0	50	10
Post Office	0	0	–74	–80	–185	–230	–210	–180	–180	0	0	0
Other[4]	–17											
Transport	**1 016**	**1 617**	**2 056**	**3 003**	**2 245**	**2 460**	**1 130**	**1 320**	**2 020**	**230**	**–820**	**–430**
Railways[5]	711	1 077	1 464	2 064	1 461	1 500	200	480	1 410	230	–770	–260
Civil Aviation Authority[6]	47	66	38	56	92	60	35	10	0	0	–5	–10
London Transport	259	474	554	883	693	900	890	820	610	0	–40	–160
DOE – Environment	**19**	**48**	**50**	**48**	**49**	**50**	**50**	**50**	**50**	**0**	**0**	**0**
British Waterways Board	47	48	50	48	49	50	50	50	50	0	0	0
Other[4]	–27											
Scotland	**–143**	**–116**	**–39**	**27**	**28**	**–30**	**–30**	**10**	**50**	**0**	**0**	**0**
Caledonian MacBrayne Ltd	6	5	9	13	12	10	10	10	10	0	0	0
Electricity (Scotland)[7]	–149	–108	–45	14	–28	–40	–40	0	40	0	0	0
Scottish Transport Group	0	–13	–2	0	44	0				0		
Agriculture, Fisheries and Food												
Other[4]	8											
Wales												
Other[4]	15											
Total[8]	**932**	**3 452**	**3 770**	**4 757**	**4 447**	**3 480**	**1 580**	**1 430**	**1 800**	**280**	**–850**	**–430**

[1] For definitions, rounding and other conventions, see notes on page 129.
[2] Future plans cover the cost of residual liabilities after privatisation.
[3] The Regional Electricity Companies, the National Grid Company, PowerGen and National Power were privatised during 1990–91. From 1991–92 comprises only Nuclear Electric.
[4] These items include the financing requirements of nationalised industries privatised before 1994–95 other than the non-nuclear electricity industries.
[5] Includes the financing requirements of British Rail, Railtrack, Union Railways and European Passenger Services and grants from the Office of Passenger Rail Franchising and Metropolitan Railway Grant (MRG). (MRG paid in Scotland is also included in the total for Scotland in Table 6.5).
[6] The total financing requirement for the Civil Aviation Authority is shown in this row. This includes subsidies from the Scottish Office Industry Department (which are included in the total for Scotland in Table 6.5). Figures for current and plan years are rounded to the nearest £5 million.
[7] Scottish Power and Scottish Hydro–Electric were privatised during 1991–92. From 1992–93 comprises Scottish Nuclear.
[8] This differs from the Nationalised Industries line of Table 6.3 because it includes central government grants from the Office of Passenger Rail Franchising and Metropolitan Railway Grant.

Table 6A.6 General government debt interest

	Outturn		Projections			
	1992–93	1993–94	1994–95	1995–96	1996–97	1997–98
	£ billion					
General government gross debt interest	17·9	19·7	22·6	25·2	26·6	26·6
of which: central government	17·4	19·2	22·1	24·5	26·0	26·2
General government interest and dividend receipts	5·2	5·1	4·2	4·6	4·8	4·7
General government net debt interest	12·7	14·5	18·3	20·5	21·7	21·8
	Percent of GDP					
General government gross debt interest	3	3	3¼	3½	3½	3¼
General government net debt interest	2	2¼	2¾	2¾	2¾	2¾

Annex B to Chapter 6
Departmental groupings

Short title used in tables	Departments covered
Defence	Ministry of Defence
Foreign Office	Foreign and Commonwealth Office – Diplomatic Wing
Overseas Development	Foreign and Commonwealth Office – Overseas Development Administration
Agriculture, Fisheries and Food	Ministry of Agriculture, Fisheries and Food The Intervention Board
Trade and Industry	Department of Trade and Industry Office of Fair Trading Office of Telecommunications Office of Electricity Regulation Office of Gas Supply
ECGD	Export Credits Guarantee Department
Employment	Department of Employment Advisory, Conciliation and Arbitration Service Health and Safety Commission
Transport	Department of Transport Office of the Rail Regulator Office of Passenger Rail Franchising
DOE – Housing	Department of Environment – Housing
DOE – Environment	Department of Environment – Other Environmental Services
DOE – PH, PSA etc	Office of Water Services Ordnance Survey Property Holdings PSA Services
DOE – Local government	Department of Environment – mainly block and transitional grants to English local authorities
Home Office	Home Office Charity Commission
Legal departments	Lord Chancellor's Department Crown Office, Scotland and Lord Advocate's Department Crown Prosecution Service Northern Ireland Court Service Public Record Office Serious Fraud Office Treasury Solicitor's Department Land Registry

Education	Department for Education
	Office for Standards in Education
National Heritage	Department of National Heritage
	Office of the National Lottery
Health	Department of Health
	Office of Population Censuses and Surveys
Social Security	Department of Social Security
Scotland	Scottish Office
	Forestry Commission
	General Register Office (Scotland)
	Scottish Courts Administration
	Scottish Record Office
	Registers of Scotland
Wales	Welsh Office
	Office of Her Majesty's Chief Inspector of Schools in Wales
Northern Ireland	Northern Ireland Office and Departments
Chancellor's departments	HM Treasury
	Central Statistical Office
	Crown Estate Office
	Department for National Savings
	Government Actuary's Department
	HM Customs and Excise
	Inland Revenue
	National Investment and Loans Office
	Registry of Friendly Societies
	Royal Mint
	Paymaster General's Office
Cabinet Office – OPSS	Office of Public Service and Science
	Central Office of Information
	Her Majesty's Stationery Office
Cabinet Office – other, etc	Cabinet Office
	House of Commons
	House of Lords
	National Audit Office
	Parliamentary Commissioner and Health Service Commissioners
	Privy Council Office
European Communities	Net payments to European Community institutions

List of abbreviations

ACT	Advance Corporation Tax
AEF	Aggregate External Finance
Blue Book	UK national accounts
CAA	Civil Aviation Authority
CAP	Common Agricultural Policy
CBI	Confederation of British Industry
CGBR	Central Government Borrowing Requirement
CGBR(O)	Central Government Own Account Borrowing Requirement
CGT	Capital Gains Tax
CSO	Central Statistical Office
CTRL	Channel Tunnel Rail Link
DBFO	Design, Build, Finance and Operate
DCS	Defence Costs Study
DOE	Department of the Environment
DSS	Department of Social Security
DTI	Department of Trade and Industry
DVLA	Driver and Vehicle Licensing Agency
ECGD	Export Credits Guarantee Department
ECU	European Currency Unit
EFL	External Financing Limits
ERM	Exchange Rate Mechanism
EU	European Union
FSBR	Financial Statement and Budget Report
G7	Major seven industrial countries
GDP	Gross Domestic Product
GGE	General Government Expenditure
GGR	General Government Receipts
GGBR	General Government Borrowing Requirement
GGBR(O)	General Government Own Account Borrowing Requirement
GGFD	General Government Financial Deficit
ICCs	Industrial and Commercial Companies
IT	Information Technology
LABR	Local Authority Borrowing Requirement
LFS	Labour Force Survey
MIPs	Mortgage Interest Payments
Money GDP	Gross Domestic Product in current market prices
MTFS	Medium-Term Financial Strategy
M0	Narrow measure of money stock
M4	Broad measure of money stock
NHS	National Health Service

List of abbreviations

NICs	National Insurance Contributions
OECD	Organisation for Economic Cooperation and Development
OPSS	Office of Public Service and Science
PAYE	Pay As You Earn
PCBR	Public Corporations Borrowing Requirement
PCMOB	Public Corporations' Market and Overseas Borrowing
PEP	Personal Equity Plan
PH	Property Holding
PRT	Petroleum Revenue Tax
PSA	Property Services Agency
PSBR	Public Sector Borrowing Requirement
PSFD	Public Sector Financial Deficit
RPI	Retail Prices Index
SAYE	Save As You Earn
SDR	Special Drawing Right
TESSA	Tax Exempt Special Savings Account
TSS	Total Standard Spending
VAT	Value Added Tax
VCT	Venture Capital Trust
VED	Vehicle Excise Duty

List of charts

		Page
1.1	Expenditure and receipts	6
1.2	Public sector borrowing requirement	6
2.1	RPI ex MIPs inflation	14
3.1	G7 GDP and world trade	19
3.2	Non-oil commodity prices	19
3.3	G7 long-term interest rates and inflation	20
3.4	GDP	21
3.5	Domestic demand, net trade and GDP	22
3.6	Personal sector consumption, income and saving	23
3.7	Housing turnover and prices	24
3.8	Housing affordability	25
3.9	The personal sector financial balance	25
3.10	Companies' real rates of return	27
3.11	Business investment/GDP ratio	27
3.12	General government fixed investment	28
3.13	Stockbuilding and GDP growth	29
3.14	Industrial and commercial companies' financial balance	30
3.15	Employment	31
3.16	Productivity	32
3.17	Unemployment	33
3.18	Competitiveness	34
3.19	Unit labour costs in manufacturing	35
3.20	Export profit margins	36
3.21	Exports and overseas demand	37
3.22	Imports and demand	37
3.23	The current account	39
3.24	Financial balances and the current account	40
3.25	Sterling exchange rate index	41
3.26	Interest rates	42
3.27	Monetary growth	43
3.28	Recent inflation indicators	44
3.29	Retail price inflation excluding MIPs	46
3A.1	Output and inflation	52

List of charts

		Page
4.1	Public sector borrowing requirement and current deficit	65
4.2	Public sector debt	66
4.3	Taxes and social security contributions	68
4.4	General government expenditure	70
4.5	Comparison of Budget projections for PSBR	71
6.1	The Control Total	110
6.2	The Control Total in real terms	111
6.3	General government expenditure (excluding privatisation proceeds)	113
6.4	General government expenditure (excluding privatisation proceeds) by function in 1993–94	113
6.5	Gross running costs of civil departments in cash terms	115
6.6	Gross running costs of civil departments in real terms	115

List of tables

		Page
1.1	The public sector's finances	5
1.2	Changes in the projections since November 1993	7
1.3	Budget changes in tax and spending	7
1.4	The Budget tax and national insurance measures	9
1.5	The public spending plans	10
1.6	The public finances in 1994–95 and 1995–96	11
3.1	The world economy	18
3.2	Gross domestic fixed capital formation at constant prices	29
3.3	Non-oil visible trade	38
3.4	The current account	39
3.5	Retail and producer output price inflation	46
3.6	Recent Treasury forecasts	47
3.7	Treasury and Independent Panel forecasts	48
3.8	Summary of economic prospects	49
3.9	Gross domestic product and its components	50
3A.1	Output growth and inflation	51
3A.2	Differences from November 1993 MTFS projections	52
3A.3	Economic assumptions for public expenditure	53
3B.1	Summary of short-term forecasts	55
3B.2	Forecasts of domestic demand	56
3B.3	Forecasts of net trade and the current account	57
3B.4	Inflation forecasts	59
3B.5	Summary of panel members' short-term forecasts	60
3B.6	Summary of panel members' medium-term forecasts	62
4.1	Public sector borrowing requirement	63
4.2	The public sector's finances	65
4.3	Public sector debt	66
4.4	General government receipts	67
4.5	General government expenditure	69
4.6	Changes since the last Budget	70
4.7	Changes in the projection of receipts	71

List of tables

		Page
4.8	Changes in the public spending projections	72
4.9	Funding requirement forecast for 1994–95	73
4.10	Variant growth projections	74
4.11	Variant PSBR projections	74
4A.1	General government receipts	76
4A.2	Public sector borrowing requirement by sector	77
4A.3	Central government transactions on a cash receipts and outlays basis	78
4A.4	Local authority transactions	79
4A.5	Public corporations' transactions	79
4A.6	Public sector transactions by sub-sector and economic category	80
4A.7	Comparison with previous forecasts	82
4A.8	Historical series for the PSBR and its components	83
4A.9	Historical series for government receipts	84
5.1	Direct effects of Budget measures	102
5B.1	Direct effect of measures announced since the November 1993 Budget	106
5B.2	Direct effect of measures announced in the November 1993 Budget or earlier which do not take effect until after the November 1994 Budget	107
6.1	The Control Total	110
6.2	Total Budget changes in public expenditure	111
6.3	The Control Total and general government expenditure (excluding privatisation proceeds)	112
6.4	Public sector capital expenditure	116
6.5	Control Total by department	119
6.6	Local authority expenditure	128
6A.1	Public expenditure, 1963–64 to 1997–98	131
6A.2	General government expenditure (excluding privatisation proceeds): plans and outturn	132
6A.3	Control Total by department	133
6A.4	Control Total by department in real terms	134
6A.5	Financing requirements of the nationalised industries, by department and industry	135
6A.6	General government debt interest	136